BEAR MARKET TRADING

Stock trading system strategies. 101 beginner's guide to learn the trading bases in Options.

LUDWIG VON MILES

LUDWIG VON MILES
© Copyright 2019 by Ludwig von Miles
All rights reserved.

This document is geared towards providing exact and reliable information with regards to the topic and issue covered. The publication is sold with the idea that the publisher is not required to render accounting, officially permitted, or otherwise, qualified services. If advice is necessary, legal or professional, a practiced individual in the profession should be ordered.

From a Declaration of Principles which was accepted and approved equally by a Committee of the American Bar Association and a Committee of Publishers and Associations.

In no way is it legal to reproduce, duplicate, or transmit any part of this document in either electronic means or in printed format. Recording of this publication is strictly prohibited and any storage of this document is not allowed unless with written permission from the publisher. All rights reserved.

The information provided herein is stated to be truthful and consistent, in that any liability, in terms of inattention or otherwise, by any usage or abuse of any policies, processes, or directions contained within is the solitary and utter responsibility of the recipient reader. Under no circumstances will any legal responsibility or blame be held against the publisher for any reparation, damages, or monetary loss due to the information herein, either directly or indirectly.

Respective authors own all copyrights not held by the publisher.

The information herein is offered for informational purposes solely, and is universal as so. The presentation of the information is without contract or any type of guarantee assurance.

The trademarks that are used are without any consent, and the publication of the trademark is without permission or backing by the trademark owner. All trademarks and brands within this book are for clarifying purposes only and are the owned by the owners themselves, not affiliated with this document.

Disclaimer

All erudition contained in this book is given for informational and educational purposes only. The author is not in any way accountable for any results or outcomes that emanate from using this material. Constructive attempts have been made to provide information that is both accurate and effective, but the author is not bound for the accuracy or use/misuse of this information.

FOREWORD

First, I will like to thank you for taking the first step of trusting me and deciding to purchase/read this life-transforming book. Thanks for spending your time and resources on this material.

I can assure you of exact results if you will diligently follow the exact blueprint, I lay bare in the information manual you are currently reading. It has transformed lives, and I strongly believe it will equally transform your own life too.

All the information I presented in this Do It Yourself piece is easy to digest and practice.

TABLE OF CONTETNS

INTRODUCTION 1

CHAPTER ONE 3
    What is Bear market?

CHAPTER TWO 15
    The fundamentals of Bear market

CHAPTER THREE 47
    How to Invest in Bear Market

CHAPTER FOUR 60
    The Examples of Bear market Investment

CHAPTER FIVE 80
    Where to Buy and Sell Bear Market Investment

CHAPTER SIX... 94
    The Common Mistakes Made by Beginners

CHAPTER SEVEN 126
    How to Succeed and Avoid Common Mistakes

CHAPTER EIGHT 134
    Tips to Become a Top Investor

CONCLUSION... 142

INTRODUCTION

Few out of every odd individual who buys and sells Bears is a Bear vendor, at any rate in the nuanced language of contributing terms. Most money related masters can be classified as one of two camps. Dependent upon the repeat in which they execute and the methodology driving their exercises, they're either "vendors" (think Gordon Gecko in the film "Cash Street") or "money related experts" (as in Warren Buffett).

Exchanging the protections exchange is the thing that could be contrasted with outstandingly instructed wagering. Anything can happen and there are basically no accreditations. Bear market can't avoid being exchanging Bears and segments of different sorts of associations and relationship at the Bear exchange. In every country, there is a Bear exchange where various associations get their offers recorded, when they coordinate required resources by strategies for offers. BEAR exchanging is never again kept to the space of the master budgetary authorities. It has transformed into an across the board enthusiasm by beginners and specialists the equivalent.

Exchanging is a game wherein you can't remain to be ordinary. An enormous number of new and natural vendors are being charged hundreds, even a large number of dollars by stunt skilled workers and self-communicated authorities for flawed Bear picking organizations and mechanical buy and sell signal generators.

Focal assessment makes the money related pro grasp the association's present organization and its circumstance in the market. It in like manner engages a monetary master to fathom if a Bear is misrepresented, disparaged or is exchanging at a sensible expense. Fundamental assessment is useful both for whole deal and transient positions. At the point when you know the nuts and bolts, you can improve your introduction by using the specific examination.

CHAPTER ONE

What is Bear market?

A Bear (generally called "offers" or "worth") is a sort of security that suggests proportionate ownership in the giving endeavour. This qualifies the financial specialist for that degree of the association's advantages and pay.

Bears are acquired and sold dominatingly on Bear exchanges, anyway there can be private arrangements likewise, and are the foundation of pretty much every portfolio. These exchanges need to fit with government rules which are expected to shield theorists from misleading practices. Genuinely, they have boated most various theories over the long haul. These endeavours can be obtained from most online Bear operators.

Associations issue (offer) Bear to raise advantages for work their associations. The holder of Bear (a speculator) has now acquired a touch of the association and has a case to a bit of its advantages and benefit. In a manner of speaking, a speculator is by and by an owner of the giving association. Ownership is constrained by the amount of offers an individual has in regard to the amount of remarkable offers. For example, if an association has 1,000 parts of Bear remarkable and one individual has 100 offers, that individual would guarantee and have assurance to 10% of the association's advantages and benefit.

Financial specialists don't have associations; they guarantee offers gave by organizations. Regardless, organizations are a remarkable sort of relationship in light of the way that the law views them as genuine individuals. By the day's end, associations report charges, can acquire, can guarantee property, can be sued, etc. The likelihood that an organization is an "individual" suggests that the organization guarantees its own special favourable circumstances. A corporate office overflowing with seats and tables have a spot with the endeavour, and not to the speculators.

This separation is huge in light of the way that corporate property is honestly detached from the property of financial specialists, which limits the commitment of both the organization and the speculator. If the organization comes up short, a judge may mastermind most of its points of interest sold – anyway your very own advantages are not in threat. The court can't oblige you to sell your offers, notwithstanding the way that the estimation of your offers will have fallen fundamentally. In like way, if a critical speculator falls flat, she can't offer the association's assets for remuneration off her leasers.

WHAT IS TRADING?

Exchange is a basic money related thought including the obtaining and selling of product and ventures, with compensation paid by a buyer to a vendor, or the exchanging of items or organizations between social events. Exchange can happen inside an economy among creators and customers. Overall exchange empowers countries to develop markets for the two product and endeavours that for the most part probably won't have been available to it. It is the inspiration driving why an American purchaser can pick between a Japanese, German, or American vehicle. Due to overall exchange, the market contains progressively significant test and in this manner, progressively forceful costs, which brings a more affordable thing home to the client.

In fiscal markets, exchanging implies the buying and selling of insurances, for instance, the purchase of Bear on the floor of the New York Bear Trade (NYSE). For extra on this kind of exchange, if it's not all that much issue see the section on 'what is a solicitation?

Negligence "hot tips." WallStreetHotShot4721 on the EZMillion$Trade dialog and the individuals who pay for bolstered advancements touting sure-thing Bears are not your colleagues, mentors or honest to goodness Wall Street aces. Guideline speaking, they are a bit of a siphon and-dump racket where darken individuals purchase bowls of offers in to some degree known, pitifully exchanged association (normally a penny Bear) and hit the web to exposure it up. As incidental theorists weight up on offers and drive the expense up, the criminals take their advantages, dump their offers and send the Bear staggering back to earth. Do whatever it takes not to empower them to fill their pockets. On the off chance that you're scanning for an ace, bookmark Warren Buffett's yearly letters to speculators for wise direction and observations on level-headed, whole deal contributing.

Keep extraordinary records for the IRS. In the event that you're not using a record that acknowledges charge favoured status — , for instance, a 401(k) or other workplace accounts, or a Roth or ordinary IRA — forces on theory increments and setbacks can get tangled. The IRS applies different guidelines and obligation rates, and requires the reporting of different structures for different sorts of intermediaries. (Here's a framework of the IRS rules for Bear handles.) Another bit of leeway of keeping incredible records is that disappointment adventures can be used to adjust the costs paid on pay through a faultless approach called charge hardship gathering.

Keep your perspective. Being a productive money related authority doesn't require finding the accompanying unprecedented breakout Bear before each other individual. At the point when you hear that XYZ Bear is adjusted for a pop, so have an immense number of master vendors and the potential likely has quite recently been assessed into the Bear. It may be past the indicate where it is conceivable make a quick turnaround advantage, yet that doesn't mean you're past the indicate where it is conceivable the social affair. Truly exceptional endeavours continue passing on financial specialist regard for an impressive period of time, which is a better than average conflict for seeing powerful contributing as a redirection and not a Hail Mary for smart riches.

Pick your exchanging associate cautiously. To exchange Bears you need an operator, yet don't just succumb to any vendor. Pick one with the terms and gadgets that best line up with your contributing style and experience. A more significant requirement for dynamic vendors will be low commissions and fast solicitation execution for time-fragile exchanges (like our picks for best online stages for dynamic sellers/casual speculators). Money related authorities who are new to exchanging should look for a speed up that can demonstrate to them the instruments of the exchange by methods for enlightening articles, online instructional activities and in-person classes (see NerdWallet's round-ups for the best delegates for juveniles). Various features to consider are the quality and availability of screening and Bear examination contraptions, in a rush alerts, straightforward solicitation segment and customer help.

In any case, the time spent in learning the basics of how to research Bears and experiencing the high focuses and depressed spots of Bear exchanging — paying little respect to whether there are a more noteworthy measure of the last referenced — is time especially spent, to the extent that you're getting a charge out of the ride and not putting any money you can't remain to lose in question.

Fundamental of securities exchange

The money related exchange is included exchanges, like the New York Bear Trade and the Nasdaq. Bears are recorded on a specific exchange, which joins buyers and vendors and goes about as a business open door for the bits of those Bears. The exchange tracks the free market movement — and genuinely related, the expense — of each Bear. (Need to back up a piece? Examine our explainer about Bears.)

Right when people suggest the money related exchange being up or down, they're all things considered implying one of the critical market records.

A market document tracks the presentation of a social affair of Bears, which either addresses the market with everything taken into account or a specific fragment of the market, like development or retail associations. You're likely going to hear most about the S&P 500, the Nasdaq composite and the Dow Jones Industrial Average; they are much of the time used as middle people for the introduction of the general market.

Examiners use records to benchmark the display of their own portfolios and, some of the time, to light up their Bear exchanging decisions. You can in like manner put assets into an entire record through document resources and exchange exchanged resources, or ETFs, which track a specific document or territory of the market.

Bear exchanging information

Most budgetary authorities would be well-taught to make an upgraded portfolio concerning Bears or Bear rundown resources and grip it through different troubles. However, money related masters who like to some degree greater movement take an interest in Bear exchanging. Bear exchanging incorporates acquiring and selling Bears a significant part of the time attempting to time the market.

The goal of Bear dealers is to misuse transitory market events to sell Bears for an advantage, or buy Bears at a low. Some Bear specialists are casual speculators, which means they buy and sell a couple of times for the term of the day. Others are simply unique specialists, putting at any rate twelve exchanges for every month.

Examiners who exchange Bears do wide research, as often as possible devoting hours day by day to following the market. They rely upon particular examination, using instruments to chart a Bear's advancements attempting to find exchanging openings and examples. Various online middle people offer Bear exchanging information, including master reports, Bear research and diagramming gadgets.

Decidedly drifting markets versus bear markets

Nor is an animal you'd have to continue running into on an ascension, yet the market has picked the bear as the authentic picture of fear: A bear market means Bear expenses are falling — limits move, anyway all things considered to the tune of 20% or more — over a couple of the records referenced previously.

Progressively energetic budgetary masters may be alright with the term bear exhibit anyway new to the experience:

We've been in an emphatically drifting business part — with increasing costs, something in opposition to a hold up under market — since March 2009. That makes it the longest bull continue running ever.

Luckily the ordinary decidedly slanting business division far outlasts the typical bear promote, which is the explanation as time goes on you can build up your money by placing assets into pillories.

The S&P 500, which holds around 500 of the greatest Bears in the U.S., has genuinely re-established a typical of around 7% consistently, when you factor in reinvested benefits and modify for development. That suggests in case you contributed $1,000 30 years back, you could have around $7,600 today.

Protections exchange crash versus cure

A protections exchange review happens when the budgetary exchange drops by 10% or more. A protections exchange crash is an unexpected, incredibly sharp drop in Bear expenses, as in October 1987, when Bears dove 23% in a single day.

While incidents can declare a bear show off, recall what we referenced above: Most determinedly floating markets last longer than bear markets — which means cash related trades will general ascending in rousing power after some time.

The criticalness of improvement

You can't keep up a fundamental decent ways from bear includes as a money related ace. What you can maintain a strategic distance from is the threat that starts from an undiversified portfolio.

Update shields your portfolio from unavoidable market difficulties. On the off chance that you fling a large portion of your cash into one affiliation, you're betting on progress that can rapidly be done by administrative issues, poor position or an E. coli eject.

To smooth out that affiliation express risk, budgetary specialists enlarge by pooling different sorts of Bears together, counterbalancing the inevitable disillusionments and taking out the peril that one affiliation's dirtied meat will crash your whole portfolio.

Regardless, creating an isolated strategy of individual Bears takes a ton of time, assurance and research. The decision is a typical spare, the as of late referenced ETF or an archive account. These hold a bushel of theories, so you're consequently extended. A S&P 500 ETF, for instance, would plan to reflect the presentation of the S&P 500 by setting resources into the 500 relationship in that record.

The lifting news is you can join individual Bears and assets in a solitary portfolio. One recommendation: Dedicate 10% or less of your portfolio to picking a few Bears you believe in, and put the rest into once-over holds.

Bit by bit directions to contribute

There are different ways for starting inspectors to purchase Bears, each with focal concentrations and preventions. In the event that you need low charges, you need to put additional time dealing with your undertakings. On the off chance that you wish to beat the market, you'll pay higher charges. On the off chance that you need a ton of exhortation, you'll need to pay even more too. On the off chance that you don't have a great deal of time or intrigue, you may need to make due with lower results.

Maybe the most hazard is from the lively bit of contributing. Most Bear purchasers get anxious when the market is progressing enjoyably. Incredibly, this makes them purchase Bears when they are the most extreme. Obviously, an insufficiently performing business portion triggers dread. That makes most cash related experts sell when the costs are low.

Picking what bearing to contribute is an individual decision. It depends upon your comfort with danger. It in like manner depends upon your ability and capacity to contribute vitality getting some answers concerning the budgetary exchange.

Purchase Bears Online

Purchasing Bears online costs the least, yet gives little exhortation. You are just charged a level expense, or a percent of your buy, for every trade. It very well may be the least secure. You clearly get practically zero exhortation. It expects you to instruct yourself altogether on the best way to contribute. Consequently, it additionally takes the most time. It's a smart thought to audit the top web based market locales before you begin.

Speculation Clubs

Joining a speculation club gives you more data at a sensible expense. Be that as it may, it takes a great deal of effort to meet with the other club individuals. They all have different degrees of mastery. You might be required to pool a portion of your assets into a club account before contributing. Once more, it's a smart thought to examine the better contributing clubs before you begin.

Full-Service Brokers

A full-administration dealer is costly on the grounds that you'll pay higher charges. Notwithstanding, you get more data and suggestions. That shields you from ravenousness and dread. You should search around to choose a decent money related proficient that you can trust. The Securities and Trade Commission offers accommodating tips on the most proficient method to choose an agent.

Cash Manager

Cash administrators select and purchase the Bears for you. You pay them a weighty charge, typically 1-2 percent of your complete portfolio. On the off chance that the chief progresses admirably, it takes minimal measure of time. That is on the grounds that you can simply meet with them more than once per year. Ensure you realize how to choose a decent monetary counsellor.

List Fund

Otherwise called trade traded assets, record assets can be a cheap and safe approach to benefit from Bears. They essentially track the Bears in a file. Models incorporate the MSCI developing business sector record. The reserve rises and falls alongside the file. There is no yearly expense. Be that as it may, it's difficult to outflank the market along these lines since record supports just track the market. All things being equal, there are a great deal of valid justifications why you ought to put resources into a file subsidize.

Common Funds

Common assets are a generally more secure approach to benefit from Bears. The store supervisor will purchase a gathering of Bears for you. You don't possess the Bear, yet a portion of the store. Most assets have a yearly expense, between 0.5 percent to 3 percent. They guarantee to outflank the S&P 500, or other equivalent file reserves. For additional, see 16 Best Tips on Mutual Fund Basics and Before You Buy a Mutual Fund.

Theoretical Bear speculations

Theoretical Bear speculations look like basic resources. Both of them pool all of their examiners' dollars into one viably supervised hold. In any case, theoretical Bear speculations put assets into ensnared fiscal instruments known as subordinates. They assurance to defeat the normal resources with these significantly used theories.

Theoretical Bear ventures are furtively held associations, not open organizations. That suggests they aren't coordinated by the SEC. They are risky, yet various examiners acknowledge this higher danger prompts a better yield.

Selling Your Bears

As huge as buying Bears is acknowledging when to sell them. Most money related authorities buy when the protections exchange is rising and sell when it's falling. Regardless, a clever examiner seeks after a strategy subject to their budgetary needs.

You should reliably watch out for the noteworthy market records. The three greatest U.S. records are the Dow Jones Industrial Average, the S&P 500, and the Nasdaq. In any case, don't solidify in case they enter a modification or a mishap. Those events don't prop up long.

On the off chance that you don't have a great deal of time to deal with your Bears, you ought to think about an overhauled portfolio. That recommends holding a reasonable blend of Bears, bonds, and things. The Bears will promise you benefit by market rises. The bonds and things shield you from downswings.

The particular blend is your bit of room task. It relies on your cash related objectives. In the event that you needn't sit around with the cash for a noteworthy timeframe, by then a higher blend of Bears will give a dynamically indisputable profit as time goes for. In the event that you require the cash one year from now, you'll need more protections.

Rebalance your portfolio two or multiple times every year. It will hence promise you purchase low and sell high. For instance, if things progress enjoyably and Bears do inadequately, your portfolio will have too high a level of things. To rebalance, you'll sell two or three things and get two or three Bears. That powers you to sell the things when costs are high and purchase the Bears when costs are low.

CHAPTER TWO

The fundamentals of Bear market

The right hypothesis demeanour, essentially, is a blend of six key characteristics. Over the long haul, it is the right contributing mentality that will have the impact between an OK examiner and a dependably productive monetary pro.

What do we fathom by the articulation "Contributing Mindset"? Essentially, it is about the mental and mental constitution of the money related master. Remember, contributing is as a lot of a mental interruption as it is a series of skill and data. To be sure, even with the best of putting aptitudes and all around data, you are most likely not going to win as a budgetary authority aside from in the event that you have the right contributing viewpoint. The right adventure standpoint, essentially, is a blend of six key characteristics. Over the long haul, it is the right contributing attitude that will have the impact between a good budgetary authority and a dependably productive examiner.

1. Mental balance is the key

   What do we fathom by mental levelheadedness? It is the ability to think indisputably despite when markets are unusual and the money related authority is under tremendous weight. Usually, this is when most monetary masters will as a rule sway and submit veritable contributing botches. Believe it or not, mental quietness is about the evening out that you can keep up despite when the market appears to strife with you. There are extremely two perspectives to mental balance. Protections exchanges are driven by fear and insatiability. Ordinarily, money related pros will when all is said in done get energetic at the most elevated purpose of the market and terrible at the base of the market. Smart contributing is connected to doing the cautious reverse. For example, if you had kept up your balance at the market lows of 2003 and 2009, by then you would have ended up with surprising hypotheses at remarkable expenses.

2. Not just tranquillity; you also require balance

   How definitely is balance novel in connection to tranquillity? What makes a difference is extremely unnoticeable anyway notwithstanding all that it exists. For example, self-restraint is connected to being terrible or greedy in the business segments at the fortunate time. If you get this mix wrong, you could end up with mishaps. Parity is about the point of view wherein you take decisions. A segment of the basic principles are: Avoid choosing huge endeavour decisions when you are in a state of ire or dissatisfaction. Similarly, avoid hypothesis decisions when you are in a state of uneasiness or stagger. Above all, keep away from taking authentic endeavour decisions in a state of vitality since you are well while in transit to overextend yourself.

3. Do whatever it takes not to seek after returns, seek after the right framework

   If you are more focused on the results rather than the technique, if you are more worried over the terminations than about the strategies, by then you have a mentality issue with respect to contributing. Remember, contributing is substantially more of getting the framework right. How you recognize Bears, how you screen Bears, what are the non-cash related parameters you consider, how might you impact on the channel and the edge of security, how might you incorporate a motivation by aligning your passage and leave levels; all these are a bit of your endeavour methodology or system. Your consideration should be on fulfilling this methodology and the results will thusly seek after.

4. Act normally decided and be a self-understudy

   The protections exchange is a remarkable teacher yet to really take in the fundamental activities from the market, you should be an excited observer and a self-moved understudy. The best way to deal with gain from the market is to listen energetically to what the market is endeavouring to tell you. Endeavor to record the learnings from the market consistently and it can transform into your Bible for exchanging. The embodiment of the issue is that your viewpoint should be that of a self-understudy. The market isn't the place you will be demonstrated the nuances. It is a monstrous gathering of data from which you can liberally draw upon.

5. Be unassuming to recognize adversities and your mistakes

   If you don't practice quietude in your exercises, by then contributing isn't for you. The best of money related authorities get their theories wrong. Attempt to be unassuming enough to yield that you weren't right and make appropriate helpful move. If gaudiness drives you to either average the position or outflank the market, by then you will have a certifiable frame of mind issue when you are contributing. Recognize that the market has a lot to demonstrate to you and recognize your mistakes. That is the route in to the right contributing attitude.

6. An ounce of movement justifies a pound of orchestrating

   You can make the best of plans on the arranging stage anyway you truly need to movement on them. There are a couple of things about the protections exchanges that you can adjust just once you start exchanging with real money. Amusement can simply take you as of not long ago! Grasp a frame of mind that is action masterminded rather than delighting a great deal in cunning. Finally, that is what makes a difference!

The 4 Different Money Mindsets of Investing

1. People Who Prefer to Give Their Investing Capital to Someone Else

   These individuals are deliberately missing about contributing in light of the way that they recognize that they are occupied with different things that are besides enchanting to them.

   In this manner, they give their cash to a common store director and take essential spare experience course from somebody who gets you a 3% return on your cash. You surely aren't getting the advantages you merit by having another person deal with your cash and you completely don't have the foggiest idea what affiliations your cash is set resources into.

2. People Who Don't Want to Learn to Invest

   They don't recognize they can do it; these individuals are purposefully careless about contributing in light of the way that they trust it's difficult to learn or not worth the exertion.

The marvellous thing about self copying benefits is that it continues working when you aren't. You need to drive a little exertion direct, yet over the long haul you essentially find the opportunity to watch your cash make in the money related trade.

3. People Who Have No Money (Or Think They Don't Have Enough Money)

   These people think they need money to be a theorist and are coincidentally absent about contributing money. You can make sense of how to contribute without a tremendous measure of money. I've clarified the most ideal approach to save $500 before if you need a lively pay lift to start contributing.

   The cash related trade recommends the party of business parts and trades where regular exercises of purchasing, selling, and issuance of bits of straightforwardly held affiliations happen. Such budgetary exercises are passed through dealt with customary trades or over-the-counter (OTC) business centres which work under a depicted plan of principles. There can be unmistakable Bearmarket settings a nation or a territory which permit trades Bears and different sorts of protections.

While the two terms - insurances trade and Bear trade - are utilized on the other hand, the last term is commonly a subset of the past. On the off chance that one says that she trades the financial trade, it derives that she purchases and sells shares/values on (in any occasion one) of the Bear trade(s) that are a touch of the general insurances trade. The essential Bear trades the U.S. combine the New York Bear Trade (NYSE), Nasdaq, the Better Alternative Market System (BATS). additionally, the Chicago Board

Options Trade (CBOE). These driving national trades, near to a few different trades working the nation, structure the cash related trade of the U.S.

Regardless of how it is known as a cash related trade or worth element and is basically known for market Bears/values, other budgetary affirmations - like trade traded assets (ETF), corporate securities and reinforcements dependent on Bears, things, monetary structures, and insurances - are additionally traded the assurances trades.

Understanding the Bear Market

While today it is conceivable to buy about everything on the web, there is consistently a consigned market for everything. For example, individuals drive to city edges and farmlands to buy Christmas trees, visit the nearby timber market to purchase wood and other essential material for home merchandise and revamps, and go to stores like Walmart for their standard basic sustenance thing supplies.

Such committed markets fill in as a stage where various purchasers and merchants meet, group up and execute. Since the measure of market people is monstrous, one is guaranteed of a reasonable cost. For instance, if there is just a single seller of Christmas trees in the whole city, he will have the chance to charge any regard he satisfies as the purchasers won't have any place else to go. In the event that the measure of tree dealers is goliath in a standard business centre, they should fight with one another to draw in purchasers. The purchasers will be devastated for decision with low-or immaculate regarding making it a reasonable market with regard straightforwardness. Without a doubt, even while shopping on the web, purchasers separate costs offered by various brokers on a practically identical shopping path or transversely over various ways to get the best arrangements, persuading the particular online sellers to offer the best cost.

A cash related trade is an equal doled out market for market different sorts of affirmations a controlled, secure and dealt with the earth. Since the assurances trade joins an enormous number of market people who wish to purchase and sell shares, it guarantees reasonable surveying practices and straightforwardness in trades. While prior securities trades used to issue and plan in paper-based physical offer affirmations, the moved PC helped cash related trades work electronically.

How the Bear Market Works?

Practically, insurances trades give a protected and composed condition where market people can execute in offers and other qualified money related instruments with sureness with zero-to low-operational peril. Working under the depicted guidelines as imparted by the controller, the budgetary trades go about as crucial markets and as optional markets.

As an essential market, the assurances trade enables relationship to issue and offer their plans to the standard open in light of the way that through the procedure of starting open duties (IPO). This movement engages relationship to raise noteworthy capital from scholars. It in a general sense gathers that an affiliation disengages itself into various offers (state, 20 million offers) and sells a touch of those offers (state, 5 million offers) to customary open at a value (state, $10 per share).

To support this method, an association needs a business focus where these offers can be sold. This business focus is given by the money related exchange. If everything goes as per the plans, the association will successfully sell the 5 million ideas at an expense of $10 per offer and accumulate $50 million worth of benefits. Money related masters will get the association shares which they can plan to hold for their favoured length, completely anticipating rising in offer expense and any potential compensation as benefit portions. The Bear exchange goes about as a facilitator for this capital raising methodology and gets a charge for its organizations from the association and its cash related accessories.

Finishing the primary run offer issuance IPO exercise called the posting methodology, the Bear exchange in like manner fills in as the exchanging stage that energizes standard obtaining and selling of the recorded offers. This contains the assistant market. The Bear exchange wins a cost for each exchange that occurs on its establishment during the discretionary market activity.

The Bear exchange bears the commitment of ensuring esteem straightforwardness, liquidity, esteem divulgence and sensible dealings in such exchanging activities. As for all intents and purposes every noteworthy security exchanges over the globe by and by work electronically, the exchange keeps up exchanging systems that beneficially manage the buy and sell orders from various market individuals. They play out the worth planning ability to empower exchange execution at a worth sensible for the two buyers and vendors.

A recorded association may similarly offer new, additional offers through various commitments at a later orchestrate, as through rights issue or through seek after on offers. They may even buyback or delist their offers. The Bear exchange empowers such exchanges.

The Bear exchange normally makes and keeps up various market-level and part unequivocal pointers, like the S&P

500 record or Nasdaq 100 document, which give a measure to pursue the improvement of the general market.

The Bear exchanges moreover keep up all association news, presentations, and budgetary uncovering, which can be typically gotten to on their official destinations. A Bear exchange in like manner supports diverse other corporate-level, exchange related activities. For instance, beneficial associations may compensate examiners by paying benefits which usually begins from a bit of the association's salary. The exchange keeps up every single such datum and may reinforce its getting ready to a certain point.

Components of a Bear Market

A protections exchange fundamentally serves the going with limits:

Sensible Dealing in Securities Transactions: Depending on the standard standards of premium and supply, the Bear exchange needs to ensure that all captivated market individuals have minute access to data for all buy and sell masterminds in like manner helping in the sensible and direct evaluating of assurances. Besides, it should moreover perform gainful organizing of fitting buy and sell orders.

For example, there may be three buyers who have put orders for acquiring Microsoft shares at $100, $105 and $110, and there may be four vendors who are glad to sell Microsoft shares at $110, $112, $115 and $120. The exchange (through their PC worked robotized exchanging systems) needs to ensure that the best buy and best sell are composed, which for this circumstance is at $110 for the given measure of exchange.

Powerful Price Discovery: Bear markets need to help a gainful segment for esteem revelation, which implies the showing of picking the right cost of a security and is ordinarily performed by assessing business segment free market action and various components related with the exchanges.

Express, a U.S.- based programming affiliation is market to a detriment of $100 and has a market capitalization of $5 billion. A news thing comes in that the EU controller has compelled a fine of $2 billion on the affiliation which on a very basic level recommends that 40 percent of the affiliation's worth might be gotten out. While the budgetary trade may have obliged a market regard degree of $90 and $110 on the affiliation's offer worth, it ought to proficiently change the reasonable market regard most outrageous to suit for the potential changes in the offer cost, else examiners may battle to trade at a reasonable cost.

Liquidity Maintenance: While getting the measure of purchasers and sellers for a specific cash related security are crazy for the money related trade, it needs to guarantee that whosoever is qualified and prepared to trade gets moment access to place orders which ought to get executed at the reasonable cost.

Security and Validity of Transactions: While more people are essential for proficient working of a market, a tantamount market needs to guarantee that all people are checked and stay unsurprising with the crucial norms and guidelines, blocking default by any of the social events. Likewise, it ought to guarantee that each and every related substance working in the market should in like way cling to the benchmarks, and work inside the legitimate structure given by the controller.

Strengthen All Eligible Types of Participants: A business centre is made by an assortment of people, which breaker publicize creators, fiscal experts, dealers, researchers, and hedgers. These people work in the assurances trade with various businesses and points of confinement. For example, a budgetary master may purchase Bears and hold them for entire arrangement spreading over different years, while a shipper may enter and leave a situation inside seconds. A market producer gives principal liquidity in the market, while a hedger may get a kick out of the chance to trade subordinates for coordinating the danger related with speculations. The budgetary trade ought to guarantee that every single such part can work splendidly satisfying their ideal occupations to guarantee the market keeps working valuably.

Theorist Protection: Along with rich and institutional budgetary authorities, an incredibly colossal number of minimal monetary pros are furthermore served by the protections exchange for their constrained amount of adventures. These examiners may have limited money related data, and may not be totally aware of the snares of placing assets into Bears and other recorded instruments.

The fundamentals of option trading

On straightforward terms, trading choices incorporate purchasing and selling choices contracts on open stock trades. It's fundamentally the same as stock trading . In spite of the fact that the goal of the administrators is to acquire benefits by purchasing shares and to sell them at a more expensive rate, administrators' options can be gotten by the buy of authoritative choices and sold at a rate higher. Additionally, moreover, investors can take a short position on a stock they accept is useless, while dealers can do likewise with options. By and by, in any case, this type of trading is considerably more broadened than value trading . To start with, the way that choices contracts can be founded on an expansive scope of hidden protections implies that there are numerous territories of the application when choosing how and where to contribute. Brokers can utilize options to hypothesize on, in addition to other things, stock value, file, cash, and specific item value developments, which speak to numerous other potential profit openings. In any case, the genuine flexibility lies in the various sorts of options that can be exchanged and in the scope of various requests that can be put. When you exchange stocks, you have two principle approaches to profit, either by getting a long position or a short position on a specific wager. On the off chance that he anticipated that individual stocks should rise, he would have a basic spot in the buy of these offers to sell them later at a more expensive rate. On the off chance that I anticipated an outright esteem, I would take a short position to purchase a short clearance of the stock in the expectation of having the option to get it at a lower cost. In trading choices, the trading mode offers more options and a lot more approaches to profit. It ought to be certain that trading choices are a significantly more mind boggling issue than stock trading and that the entire idea of what this suggests may appear to be extremely demoralizing to novices. In fact, there are numerous things you have to learn before you start and contribute your cash. In any case, remembering this, most nuts and bolts are not so difficult to get it. When you know the fundamentals, it turns out to be a lot more clear what the trading choices are. The following are completely clarified. Selling and composing option; You can sell discretionary contracts in two different ways. Initially, in the event that you have just purchased the agreements and need to make a benefit or lessen the misfortunes, you will sell them by putting them marked down to close the request. The request is called all things considered on the grounds that it shuts its situation by selling discretionary contracts. By and large, he would utilize this request on the off chance that he expanded the worth he had and needed to succeed around then, or if the choices were decreased in worth and he needed to leave his situation before he made another misfortune. Another approach to sell choices is to open a position and undercut. It is otherwise called composition options in light of the fact that the procedure includes composing new contracts exchanged the market. For this situation, you will go into a legally binding commitment, that is, in the event that the proprietor utilizes his choice, at that point he should sell the hidden security at the executable cost (on the off chance that it is a buy option) or buy their fundamental worth. At the official cost (if the schedule is a choice). The composition choices have been made utilizing a business request to open them, and you get an instalment when the solicitation is submitted. When all is said in done, it's less secure than purchasing and selling, however you can profit in the event that you realize what you're doing. You would regularly request such a request in the event that you accept that the basic security intrigue would not be lost so the proprietor could exploit its capacity to acquire benefits. For instance, in the event that you believe that a few stocks will stay static or will lose esteem, at that point you can sell and trade call options dependent on this stock. You would be obligated for potential misfortunes if the estimation of the offers expanded, however on the off chance that you didn't do as endless supply of the options, you would hold the instalment you got for their composition. Purchasing options; The buy of an agreement choice practically speaking is the same than the buy of offers. In this choice, you take a long position until it increments. You can buy an agreement option by simply picking what you need to purchase and how much, and after that submitting a buy request to open a record with a representative. This order is called all things considered in light of the fact that it opens the position through the buy choices. On the off chance that your choices increment in worth, you can sell them or exercise your decision as per what suits you best. Afterward, we will give more data on the deal and utilization of options. One of the basic advantages of a choice contract is that you can get them in circumstances where you anticipate that the basic resources should increment, just as when you anticipate that the fundamental property should increment. Question be diminished. On the off chance that you intend to expand the estimation of the basic resource, you will buy call options giving you the privilege to purchase the property at a fixed cost. In the event that you were anticipating a decrease in the estimation of the basic resources, at that point you should buy the venture choices, which gives you the privilege to sell the fundamental property at a fixed cost. This is only one case of the adaptability of these agreements; There are some others If you recently opened a short position in choice decreases by keeping in touch with them, you can purchase these agreements and close this position. To close the circumstance by acquiring an arrangement, you should demand a buy to close the record with the intermediaries. Choices spread; This makes trading options an energizing method to put resources into the plausibility of making separation choices. Obviously, you can make cash purchasing openings, and after that sell them in the event that you make a benefit, however spreads are the most useful asset in the store. The range is very straightforward when you enter a situation in at least two options contracts dependent on the equivalent hidden security; for instance, buy choices for a specific stock, just as composing offers in a similar activity. You can make various kinds of separation and use them for different reasons. As a rule, they restricted the danger of obtaining or decreasing the monetary costs required to fill the position. Most business choices incorporate the utilization of differentials. A few methodology can be exceptionally muddled, yet there are likewise fundamental systems that are sensible and straightforward. Practicing choices; Opportunities Traders will in general make benefits by purchasing, selling, and composing options and never truly acknowledge them. Be that as it may, contingent upon the procedures you use, and why you obtained explicit contracts, you may utilize options to purchase or sell the fundamental security. The basic actuality that you can possibly win with the activity, just as for the buy and deal, is utilized to delineate all the adaptability and flexibility offered by this type of trading . The advantage of trading choices; This type of business offers a few points of interest, with the assortment that we referenced previously. Its notoriety keeps on developing, among expert administrators as well as among progressively casual administrators. Nuts and bolts of trading choices; Trading choices give us a lot of influence. Think about a water skier behind the vessel, and the driver should simply turn the directing wheel a piece and dispatch it at full speed or think about it. Along these lines, in specialized terms, the bit of leeway is to utilize a little exertion to move an enormous article. From a budgetary perspective, this has the impact of controlling considerably more huge ventures or resources or acquiring an exceptionally exceptional yield with a limited quantity of cash. From our own involvement, uncultivated use or abuse of the switch can be dangerous. Any speculation procedure is high hazard in the event that you don't have a clue what you are doing. Your "chance" when trading on a stock trade implies the likelihood of the blessing (misfortune) of your trading capital. A typical misstep with the investment opportunities/choices is that its utilization conveys an exceptionally high hazard.

By selling with stocks, you can endure and grow your accumulation, however you can likewise fence choices with choices to decrease potential misfortunes and even support, or offer investment opportunities! Investment opportunities are a substantially more progressed monetary instrument than values and can procure you returns paying little heed to showcase bearing or conditions. Be that as it may, similarly as you run a possibly high hazard on the off chance that you drive a vehicle without a safety belt, in the event that you don't pursue the standards when utilizing influence or stock trading , you might be presented to similar chances. Be that as it may, when power is enough regarded and used, exchange can be more secure than stock trading . Focal points or Disadvantages of Options trading ; You can draw up locales giving anything from fundamental definitions to those professing to make you wealthy in a brief period. Be cautious about those offering brisk wealth. Like they state, If it sounds unrealistic, it most likely is. Without a doubt, some have the understanding that enables them to reliably contribute their cash through options procedures and acknowledge predominant returns inside a generally brief time allotment, yet you should understand that they have been doing this long enough to realize what they are doing. Furthermore, in the event that you ask them, they would reveal to you that they made a lot of losing exchanges when they originally began learning the business. (Ideally, they paper exchanged from the start so they could learn with phony cash.) I have realized some who got inspired by choices trading and made winning exchanges ideal out of the door. Obviously, they quickly thought this was a simple method to profit and after that put an enormous part of their capital into the following exchange - just to lose huge. The lesson of the story is; on the off chance that you intend to pick your exchanges, do your exploration and recognize what you are getting yourself into. Never expect you have the market made sense of, it will humble you in the long run. All in all, what are the focal points or inconveniences of trading choices? The influence referenced frequently would presumably be the manner in which choices enable you to use your cash. For instance, on the off chance that you have $1,000 to contribute, and you need to get some XYZ stock that is trading at $100 per share, you would most likely purchase ten offers. Or on the other hand, you could take that equivalent $1,000 and put it in 5 choices contracts, enabling you to control 500 offers rather than only 10. (Keep in mind, with choices, each agreement controls 100 offers.) So, on the off chance that you purchased the ten portions of stock and the stock worth increments by $1.00 per share, you increase an entire $10.00. However, on the off chance that you obtained the five options contracts and the worth expanded by .20 pennies, you would understand an addition of $100 (.20 x 500 offers). Another favourable position is its adaptability. With that, I figure you can profit on bullish, bearish or remote markets. Keep in mind that before moving to exchange choices, you have to see how they work and what systems to use at the perfect time. Without going into subtleties, get the job done it to state that in the event that you anticipate that the stock's worth should build, purchase the call option. On the off chance that you expect a lower value, purchase a movement choice. Purchase and sell options are the most fundamental sorts exchanged and convey dangers. Numerous procedure options can be extremely confused, so recall moral stories: on the off chance that you intend to pick your tasks, investigate and recognize what you are taking part in. This article isn't planned to energize or dishearten you from entering the universe of trading choices. Additionally, it is composed to show a portion of its advantages, featuring the truth of its dangers. On the off chance that this speculation course is energizing and you need to attempt it, we can offer you a spot where an accomplished broker picks his tasks. So far this year, in 2008, our ventures have created an arrival on speculation above 100%. Visit our site and get familiar with our administrations. Disclaimer: The trading of monetary instruments of any sort, including choices, bonds, and protections, has impressive potential advantages, yet additionally a critical potential hazard. You have to know the dangers and be eager to acknowledge them to put resources into options, awards, and grants. Try not to deal with cash you cannot lose. Nothing in this article ought to be understood as a bit of speculation exhortation or suggestion. Results so far show future outcomes. Get help from a skilled budgetary guide before putting your cash in a money related instrument. For our supporters, we send option exchanges that we enter, just as when we leave activities. We offer an option for the individuals who don't have opportunity to do specialty look into. Over the most recent three years, we have won a record.

Choice Trading Strategy, in the realm of fund, is the deal or buy of one or different option positions and conceivably a basic zone. There are various Stock Option Trading Strategies to browse. The amazing methodology is to gain proficiency with the essential bull call spread and after that adapt progressively complex systems each one in turn. Investment opportunities are the same with other speculation which you can apply different procedures. These may run from the most moderate to intense. In the last examination, you should choose what sort of speculator you are. Is it accurate to say that you are the sort of financial specialist who needs to be wary of your speculations to save gains or a remarkable inverse which is prepared to go out on a limb to acquire? By the by, regardless of what sort of financial specialist you are, the essential objective is to pick up benefits. This may require incessant market checking so you can pick the technique that matches the market and along these lines, increment your odds of gaining benefits. Systems are arranged into gatherings, for example, vertical spreads, delta spreads, proportion spreads, and credit spreads. Various methodologies work for various types of business sectors. For example, a vertical range straddles or choke system can be used to further your potential benefit in either a bull or bear advertise. Of course, a proportion spread is a valuable technique for a market going sideways. There are various varieties of procedures: · Ratio Spreads utilize an odd number of short and long protections to balance chance. · Vertical Spreads or cash spreads choices of the equivalent basic security, same termination months yet at various strike costs. · Credit spread sells an option position that is close to the present market while purchasing a choices position that is further from the market yet a comparative way. · Delta spread makes an unbiased position by considering the deltas of the choices. The delta of choice acquired is separated by delta of the choice composed Variations inside the methodologies are likewise accessible. You will discover a few strategies, that is the reason investment opportunities trading is viewed as one of the most complex venture techniques. For example, vertical spreads may include: Bear put spreads where the financial specialist is purchasing an option at or close to the cash than the choice that is shorted. Bull call spreads, then again, is the inverse.

This is one of the most widely recognized bought ranges that includes purchasing a call choice at a lesser strike cost while selling a call option at a higher strike cost. Hazard inversion spread is a forceful spread system that unions an extraordinary option and a short choice so that the two choices can profit by the equivalent directional development of the fundamental fates. Different systems you can utilize incorporate the proportion put spread, proportion call spread, the back spread, butterfly spread, long choke, short chokes, long straddles, short straddles, and condor spread. Before you connect with yourself in this sort of speculation, you have to get familiar with the most fundamental technique like the bull call spread and afterward get familiar with the more advanced system each one in turn. In this way, start your speculation directly by setting aside the effort to peruse and choose which venture techniques would suit you. The choice is a well known subordinate since its cost is lower than other subsidiary, for example, future. Blue chip stock is an exceptionally unpredictable stock, however it is exorbitant. Be that as it may, by purchasing the option of the blue-chip stock, we could gain benefit just also like acquiring the stock. Contributing and trading option is by all accounts exceptionally simple, much the same as purchasing stock. In any case, because of the presence of time esteem and furthermore the lapse date of the chance, buying a bare option is perilous. This is provided that the stock cost is going down a great deal soon after you have acquired the stripped choice, after a specific period, despite the fact that the stock cost has gone up, the option cost may in any case underneath the asking value that you have used to purchase this choice. That why we need a system to contribute or exchange choice. A choice is an intense instrument in contributing and trading stock. By using choice, we could win benefit from the capital that moves upside, drawback, and sideways. In addition, the plausibility likewise could be utilized to execute an exchange procedure to make a benefit regardless of the stock cost is going up, down or sideways. The back spread is one of the option trading methodologies that are very mainstream. This technique is very like Chinese betting called of all shapes and sizes. In this betting, when we stake enormous and the three dices after shook and opened demonstrate the all out point is noteworthy, we will win one overlap of the cash that we have staked. That implies in the event that we stake 100, we will get back one increasingly 100. Be that as it may, in the event that we lose, we will drop 100. Back spread technique is very like this betting game. That implies on the off chance that we contribute USD 1000, we either get back one more USD 1000 or misfortune USD 1000 that has been staked in. The most extreme benefit and misfortune are USD 1000. That has fixed. You won't lose more than that. The back spread is the inversion of the ordinary range. The most extreme benefit and misfortune are not generally the equivalent. Now and again, it will vary a tad and rely upon the present cost of the stock. This procedure could be executed by purchasing an out-of-the-cash option and selling an in-the-cash choice. Since the cost of the in-the-cash choice is more than the out-of-the-cash choice, the measure of cash that has been gotten subsequent to selling in-the-cash option will be sufficient to purchase the out-of-the-cash choice. Albeit like this, despite everything we have to place a measure of store in our trading account and the sum generally is comparable to the greatest misfortune that you could cause if the stock cost goes to the turnaround heading. In this way, on the off chance that we are expecting the stock cost will go up in no time, we should purchase out-of-the-cash and in-the-cash put choice. On the other hand, on the off chance that we are expecting the stock cost will go down rapidly, we should buy out-of-the-cash and in-the-cash call choice. Only for straightforward, we attempt a model. The table underneath demonstrates a rundown of put options for MMM organization stock, which will lapse on Apr 07. Table 1: List of put choices for MMM organization stock. The present cost of the stock is USD 80.94. A put choice with its strike value more than current cost is an in-the-cash choice, and not exactly current cost is an out-of-the-cash option. In the event that we are expecting the stock cost will go up in a matter of seconds, we will get one contract of 80 put choice (MPP) and sell one contract of 85 put option (MNZPQ). When we sell a choice, we will get a measure of cash that is equal to the offered cost duplicating with the quantity of units that has been acquired. The measure of cash that has been gotten per unit choice is USD 5.2, and the measure of cash that we have to pay per unit option when we purchase out-of-the-cash choice is USD 2.7. Thusly, the net sum in your trading account in the wake of executing this technique is USD 2.5 per unit option. That implies there will be a USD 250 net in your trading account. The most extreme benefit and misfortune are determined as pursue: Maximum benefit = In-the-cash option offer cost - Out-of-the-cash choice ask value Maximum misfortune = (upper-level strike cost - lower level strike cost) - (In-the-cash choice offer cost - Out-of-the-cash choice ask value) The upper-level strike cost is 85, and the lower level strike cost is 80. In-the-cash choice offer cost is USD 5.2, and the out-of-the-cash ask cost is USD 2.7. In the wake of substituting all qualities into the conditions above, we will realize that the most extreme benefit is USD 2.5 and the greatest misfortune is likewise USD 2.5. In this way, in the event that we get one gets each of the in-the-cash and out-of-the-cash option, the greatest benefit is USD 250, and the most extreme misfortune is additionally USD 250. The make back the initial investment point for this procedure could be determined utilizing condition as pursue: Breakeven point = Upper-level strike cost - most extreme benefit Or Breakeven point = Lower level strike cost + greatest misfortune. For this situation, the breakeven point is 82.5. For whatever length of time that the stock cost goes up more than 82.5, we will procure a benefit from this methodology. We possibly could make the most extreme benefit in the event that we keep the situation until the lapse date. In the event that we auction right on time before the termination date, we couldn't gain the greatest advantage. Be that as it may, despite everything we can profit however with somewhat lesser than if we could keep the situation until the termination date. This is because of the fragmented picking up of the time estimation of the auction in-the-cash option. Along these lines, by using this options trading technique, you could acquire a benefit as long as your forecast precision is more than 50 %. That implies you must be precise for at any rate six wagers inside ten wagers. From here, the most extreme persistent misfortune is multiple times.

Along these lines, so you won't lose all your cash until you couldn't keep on wagering, you need to keep four back up measures of cash or more. In this way, on the off chance that you lose one wager, despite everything you have the cash to consistently stake for the following possibility. Like this, as long as you could keep your forecast exactness more than 50 %, your instalment will persistently develop along the time.

Most of options lapse uselessly. When you purchase an option, time is neutralizing you since you just possess a constrained measure of energy at the cost of the hidden to move quick enough and far enough to expand the estimation of the choice. You could be right toward the market and still observe your choices lose esteem in light of the fact that the market did not move quick enough. To profit when purchasing choices, you not just require the market cost to progress to support you, you need it to do as such with great instability, and you need it to do so some time before lapse. The closer the option reaches an end, the quicker it loses an incentive because of time disintegration. The motivation behind why many purchase options is that you can just lose the sum you paid for the chance.

What's more, on the off chance that you get the course right and the market moves quick enough, and soon enough, you can value your venture superior to had you chance the capital in the out and out buy of the fundamental security. On the other side, on the grounds that most options turn out useless come lapse, merchants may pick to sell choices. As a dealer of the chance, you get paid forthright for the estimation of the option as premium. Furthermore, since the chances support the choice losing esteem, many have observed offering choices to be very productive. Be that as it may, the issue with selling choices is that if some occasion moves the market quick for the choice purchaser, the choice dealer needs to cover the choice when worked out. The hazard to the option dealer is hypothetically boundless. Selling choices isn't for the black out of heart or the unpractised. Be that as it may, consider the possibility that you could have it both ways. At the end of the day, consider the possibility that you could in any case get paid a credit forthright for putting on an option exchange and advantage from time disintegration, much the same as a choice merchant, however with restricted, characterized chance. Presenting the Short Vertical Spread Strategy. Building this spread is finished by utilizing either two call options or two put choices. One of the options is sold, and the other is purchased. To cause this spread to give credit, the sold option will be the choice with the strike value that is nearer to the present rate, while the obtained choice will have a strike value that is more remote away. Since the choice with the strike progressively personal to the present cost will be more profitable than the one more distant away, you will get more premium for the one you sold than what you needed to pay for the one you purchased. Settling on whether to utilize two puts or two calls will rely upon whether you are somewhat bullish or somewhat bearish, individually. Assume that you are somewhat bullish. Assume likewise that the present cost of the hidden security is at $30. The $25 put option has an estimation of $1.60, and the estimation of the $22.50 put choice has an expense of $0.95. In the event that you sell the 25 put for a credit of $1.60 and purchase the 22.5 put option for $.95, you will wind up with an all out credit of $.65. In this model, the most that you can make on this exchange is $.65 while the most you can lose is $1.85 ($25 - $22.5 contrast in strike cost = 2.5) - $.65 you got in premium forthright. For investment opportunities where each agreement speaks to 100 offers, you would chance $185 to make $65. Presently you may feel that gambling $185 to make $65 isn't sensible hazard/remunerate, yet you have to take a gander at it along these lines. On the off chance that the exchange works out, you would then make 35% on your venture. Well that is not very ratty! There is more than you should comprehend about this spread. Assume that you are somewhat bearish and have sold and purchased a call option to put on this spread. On the off chance that value transcends the strike of the call choice you sold however not the one you bought, the purchaser of that choice could practice it and you would be required to give the purchaser the offers. On the off chance that you don't officially possess the stock, you will wind up being short 100 portions of stock. On the off chance that this transpires, however to cover your short position. You can contact your agent for help on the best way to best deal with this. On the off chance that the value moves past the strike of the two choices, your agent will treat it. Your record will be deducted the measure of misfortune, as referenced previously. There is substantially more you ought to learn before trading this technique. For instance, how to exit before lapse if quite possibly cost might travel through the strike cost before expiry, enabling you to perhaps keep most or a portion of the credit contingent upon the unpredictability of the market. With a short vertical spread (a.k.a. credit spread), time is your most noteworthy partner. What's more, if the market moves your favoured way, or next to no against you, you beat the competition. When you can profit with restricted hazard for being even a slight bit wrong in what you anticipate that the market should do, it is surely a system worth learning. In spite of the fact that purchasing a call choice and selling a put spread are bullish choices techniques, their particular Greeks profiles are extraordinary. What are the Greeks? In the first place, this word is right in the expert options trading world. We are not alluding to individuals from Greece. Rather, we are discussing the various factors that would influence an options position. Consequently, the word is "Greeks". A broker profits from purchasing a call choice on the off chance that he is directly toward the path, and the call choice turns out to be progressively costly because of an ascent in the suggested unpredictability. In any case, he can't trust that these things will happen in light of the fact that a call choice has time rot that neutralizes him. Then again, a dealer profits from selling a put spread that is out of the cash ("OTM") for the most part in view of the time rot (as time works for him in this procedure). In any case, here is a basic test. As the exchange is drawing nearer to the termination, it will be progressively touchy to any potential stock value development. That is the genuine danger of this system and thusly experienced brokers will for the most part repurchase the spread for a little premium to close the position as opposed to holding the range till termination. In this part, I will talk about the utilization of a short vertical spread for bearish plays. For this situation, we will sell an OTM call spread. To develop this spread, we will sell a call at a lower strike and purchase another call at a higher assault utilizing a similar lapse month. Like selling an OTM put spread, the top notch we gather from the sell leg is more than the superior we pay for the purchase leg. Therefore, we will get a net credit. Keep in mind, in the past part, and I said that there was no free lunch. A short call spread is additionally not a hazard organized commerce. Give me a chance to delineate this with the accompanying model. XYZ (a speculative organization) is right now trading at $500 per share. Tom (a theoretical broker) does not accept that XYZ will exchange above $500 for the following 30 days. He has along these lines developed an OTM call spread by selling 510 calls and purchasing 515 calls utilizing a similar lapse month. Suppose the net credit gotten by Tom is $150 per choice contract. Here is the means by which the hazard and reward of this technique are resolved: The most extreme honour is $150 as this is the net credit gotten by Tom The greatest hazard is $350 as this is spoken to by the contrast between the strikes

($5) x 100 less the net credit got ($150). As should be obvious, this exchange has hazard. In the event that Tom is dead off-base, his most extreme presentation will be $350 per option contract. As on account of a short put spread, the aggregate of the most extreme reward and greatest hazard is constantly equivalent to the contrast between the strikes duplicated by 100. Tom will most likely keep the whole credit of $150 if the two legs lapse OTM at termination. Since the most extreme hazard is higher than the net credit got, the genuine test of a short call spread is likewise the exchange the board, and what I talked about in Part I would be relevant here as well. Since I have examined the short put spread and the snappy call spread, you may most likely ask whether we can consolidate the two territories into a solitary exchange. The appropriate response is yes since this is the manner by which an iron condor and an iron butterfly are made. Basically, these two techniques are developed utilizing an OTM short put spread and an OTM speedy call spread. There are three essential kinds of options systems, and the fall under the classes of bullish, bearish, and unbiased.

At the point when financial specialists initially get into options, they more often than not begin with bullish choices methodologies. There is more than one sort of bullish technique, and the different kinds can be classified by how hopeful they are. Some are somewhat bullish, others respectably in this way, while the long call is the most bullish of all. Of the numerous systems accessible to financial specialists, the long call is presumably the most outstanding. This is on the grounds that most new financial specialists begin utilizing this methodology. A long call is utilized when a financial specialist predicts an ascent in the estimation of a benefit. The long solicitation is viewed as the most bullish of choices procedures, and is simple for new brokers to comprehend, which makes it available for newcomers to the market. Bull spreads, which are respectably bullish options techniques, requires somewhat more learning. These spreads utilize a mix of a long call with a short put to make an exchange that spreads out the expense of the speculation. The long consider utilizes a higher strike cost, while the long put is set at a lower strike cost. The two choices are on a similar stock. Bull spreads can likewise utilize different kinds of exchanges. These are known as vertical spread procedures and are utilized in both bullish and bearish markets. In a somewhat bullish system, the broker can make a benefit insofar as there is no genuine drop in the estimation of the advantage fundamental the choice while the option can be worked out. These choices systems are regularly utilized by scholars, or vender, of option. For new speculators in the options showcase, choices methodologies utilizing spreads might be excessively confused, however given sufficient opportunity and practice with trading choices, it is conceivable to begin adding them to your collection. Every single new financial specialist are ideal, in the first place, basic methodologies and work their way into the more entangled ones as they increase a superior comprehension of how choices trading capacities. Bullish options methodologies, similar to any venture, accompany certain dangers. There are fluctuating degrees of the hazard, similarly as there are various degrees of benefit to be had. When getting into choices trading , utilizing bullish techniques is an incredible method to begin; yet essentially on the grounds that numerous financial specialists do begin there doesn't mean it's the main spot to start. Converse with a speculation counsellor pretty much all the potential methodologies when you are prepared to begin. In spite of the fact that choices trading is frequently viewed as dangerous (and it absolutely can be), it is commonly both more secure and substantially more gainful than stock trading . The delightful thing about options trading is that takes into consideration a wide assortment of methodologies to be built up that all have distinctive hazard profiles. Despite the fact that specialist charges for choices trading are fundamentally higher than those for practically some other sort of trading , this is effectively balanced by the significant productivity accessible. The reason that choices trading has pulled in the notoriety of being too hazardous is that numerous merchants, driven by unadulterated eagerness, have attempted to accomplish most extreme returns in the base time. Madly enormous benefits are conceivable, however when dealt with an avarice thought process, crash-and-consumes are inescapable. The way to effective options trading is to "claim" a procedure, to know it personally, and to utilize it reliably and with obviously characterized trading rules. These are (as I would see it) the most perfect options trading techniques that limit hazard and give entirely good benefits: Selling Credit Spreads - with no work, and around 30 minutes per week, it is conceivable to develop your portfolio by 10-15% consistently. Achievement relies upon straightforwardness, and this is certainly not a system reasonable for hyperactive dealers or the individuals who love to over investigate everything. All you have to know is the way to complete basic pattern investigation available and your gathering of painstakingly chosen stocks. This procedure is entirely beneficial and is more agreeable than tumbling off a bull at a rodeo (and substantially less agonizing). You are selling Naked Puts. This procedure just works in an upward inclining business sector and has a to some degree higher edge necessity than that of credit spreads. You can get comparative returns, and the hazard profile is similarly as low. Interestingly, similar to credit spreads, you get your benefit in advance. You are purchasing and selling DITM (Deep-in-the-cash) choices. This is an incredible swing trading methodology and empowers you to purchase stocks at about deep discounted successfully, thus twofold your benefit. Since your exchanges are altogether present moment (3-10 days), you are not worried about profits or different variables identifying with purchasing and holding stocks, yet you do profit in light of the fact that the value development of the capital correctly coordinates the value development of the option that you obtained. Selling Covered Calls - on the off chance that you possess a stock, you can successfully decrease the expense of that stock by selling secured approaches that stock each month. This is a methodology that stock dealers ought not be managing without, yet don't utilize it on the off chance that you claim stock for nostalgic reasons - stock trading must be your business. In this way, on the off chance that you once in a while get got out and wind up selling your stock, you can rapidly proceed onward to the following one. Complex techniques, similar to straddles, chokes, iron condors and butterflies. These are largely generally safe, profoundly gainful systems. Their lone inconveniences are that they are on the whole costly (either costly options, or higher merchant expenses in view of the quantity of exchanges included).

The most effective method to trade option trading

An option trading rolling system is where you move your strike point to another strike point during the month. Moving essentially means moving. In the realm of choices trading , this development happens when you move positions starting with one strike point then onto the next. That can either happen when you move focuses vertically (around the same time) or evenly (to one more month) or both.

In request to expand returns, speculators should utilize the secured consider system consistently for quite a while. That necessitates that the speculator move, or roll, the strike position when the option terminates. That is the place the expression "moving" originates from.

Some portion of options trading moving methodology additionally includes realizing when to abstain from rolling, however. Once in a while a speculator may choose not to roll the strike position. The motivation behind that is to enable the money to acknowledge more. That is an uncommon situation, in any case, in light of the fact that, if the call option is practiced when offer moves toward becoming in the cash, it could be summoned.

As an option trading draws near, there can be both of two results. Either the short choice could be out-of-the-cash or in-the-cash. In the event that the choice is out-of the-cash, it is useless. The financial specialist essentially sells the following month's call, subsequent to allowing them to option lapse. In the event that, then again, the choice winds up in-the-cash, so as to keep the stock the financial specialist should simply sell the following month's call subsequent to repurchasing the short option. Despite the fact that that kind of exchange comprises of two exchanges, purchasing and selling, it is viewed as one exchange. It is otherwise called a spread. In the event that you need to reveal your secured call or purchase compose, you have to use such a spread. That way, you can repurchase the short option and keep your stock.

Your second month choice would be undercuts. In this manner, your secured call procedure would be re-started. The rest of the positions are the short calls and long stock. You need to repurchase the option that you are short toward the start of the month. You would not have a decision for your front month choice. Be that as it may, you would have the decision to sell close to term or with a more distant termination date for the following month option.

As should be obvious, rolling can be somewhat confused. Notwithstanding, you may think that its well justified, despite all the trouble, over the long haul. Try to be mindful so as to settle on the most educated choices conceivable. Make sure to never chance beyond what you can bear to lose either. All things considered, it's anything but a careful science.

Along these lines, since you comprehend the choices trading moving technique better, you might need to think about it. There is something to be said for utilizing choices trading moving system to improve your gaining potential, all things considered.

CHAPTER THREE

How to Invest in Bear Market

For instance, a Bear exchange may orchestrate Bears in various pieces depending upon their danger profiles and license compelled or no exchanging by standard examiners in high-chance Bears. Backups, which have been portrayed by Warren Buffett as money related weapons of mass demolition, are not for everyone as one may lose altogether more than they bet for. Exchanges consistently power constraints to foresee individuals with obliged compensation and gaining from getting into dangerous bets of auxiliaries.

Balanced Regulation: Listed associations are, as it were, controlled and their dealings are checked by advertise controllers, like the Securities and Trade Commission (SEC) of the U.S. Moreover, exchanges in like manner order certain necessities – like, promising archiving of quarterly money related reports and minute uncovering of any significant progressions - to ensure all market individuals become aware of corporate happenings. Powerlessness to hold quick to the rules can incite suspension of exchanging by the exchanges and other disciplinary measures.

Dealing with the Bear Market

A close by budgetary controller or dexterous cash related expert or foundation is doled out the task of dealing with the protections exchange of a country. The Securities and Trade Commission (SEC) is the managerial body blamed for coordinating the U.S. protections exchanges. The SEC is a managerial office that works independently of the lawmaking body and political weight. The crucial the SEC is communicated as: "to guarantee monetary authorities, take care of sensible, conscious, and gainful markets, and energize capital advancement."

Protections exchange Participants

Nearby whole deal money related masters and transient vendors, there are different sorts of players related with the protections exchange. Each has an uncommon activity, anyway countless the occupations are interlaced and depend upon each other to make the market run effectively.

- Bear brokers, generally called enrolled assigns in the U.S., are the approved specialists who buy and sell assurances to assist budgetary authorities. The vendors go about as agents between the Bear exchanges and the money related experts by obtaining and selling Bears for the theorists' advantage. A record with a retail authority is relied upon to get to the business areas.
- Portfolio boss are specialists who contribute portfolios, or gatherings of securities, for clients. These heads get proposition from examiners and choose the buy or sell decisions for the portfolio. Regular store associations, common assets, and annuity plans use portfolio chiefs to choose decisions and set the theory methods for the money they hold.

- Investment merchants address associations in various breaking points, for instance, exclusive organizations that need to open up to the world by methods for an IPO or associations that are locked in with pending mergers and acquisitions. They manage the posting method in consistence with the regulatory requirements of the budgetary exchange.
- Custodian and station authority associations, which are establishment holding customers' assurances for supervision so as to restrict the threat of their robbery or setback, also work in a condition of concordance with the exchange to move offers to/from the specific records of executing social occasions reliant on exchanging on the protections exchange.
- Market maker: A market maker is a dealer merchant who empowers the exchanging of offers by posting offer and ask costs close by keeping up a load of offers. He ensures satisfactory liquidity in the market for a particular (course of action of) share(s), and profits by the qualification between the offer and the ask esteem he refers to.

First clearance of Bear (IPO) or budgetary exchange dispatch is a kind of [public offering] in which segments of an association are offered to institutional examiners and when in doubt furthermore retail (solitary) theorists; an IPO is supported by at any rate one endeavour banks, who in like manner plan the ideas to be recorded on in any event one Bear exchanges. Through this methodology, calmly known as floating, or opening up to the world, a covertly held association is changed into an open association. Beginning open commitments can be used: to raise new esteem capital for the association stressed; to adjust the theories of private speculators, for instance, association creators or private worth money related authorities; and to enable straightforward exchanging of existing belongings or future capital raising by twisting up exchanged on an open market attempts.

After the IPO, shares exchanged wholeheartedly in the open market are known as the free skim. Bear exchanges stipulate a base free float both in incomparable terms (the full scale a motivation as constrained by the offer cost expanded by the amount of offers offered to general society) and as a degree of the hard and fast offer capital (i.e., the amount of offers offered to the open isolated by the total offers amazing). Disregarding the way that IPO offers various points of interest, there are in like manner basic costs included, transcendently those related with the methodology, for instance, banking and genuine costs, and the nonstop essential to reveal critical and at times sensitive information.

Nuances of the proposed offering are revealed to potential purchasers as an extended report known as an arrangement. Most associations endeavour an IPO with the assistance of a hypothesis banking firm acting in the point of confinement of an underwriter. Agents give a couple of organizations, joining help with precisely reviewing the estimation of offers (share cost) and working up an open market for offers (early on bargain). Elective systems, for instance, the Dutch closeout have furthermore been explored and associated for a couple of IPOs.

An association masterminding an IPO will consistently pick an underwriter or agents. They will in like manner pick an exchange where the offers will be given and along these lines exchanged straightforwardly.

The term first closeout of Bear (IPO) has been a mainstream articulation on Wall Street and among money related masters for a serious long time. The Dutch are credited with coordinating the chief present day IPO by offering segments of the Dutch East India Company to the general populace. Starting now and into the foreseeable future, IPOs have been used as a course for associations to raise capital from open budgetary masters through the issuance of open offer belonging. As the years advanced, IPOs have been known for rises and downtrends in issuance. Solitary fragments moreover experience rises and downtrends in issuance due to progression and diverse other money related parts. Tech IPOs copied at the height of the site impact as new organizations without livelihoods rushed to show themselves on the budgetary exchange. The 2008 budgetary crisis realized a year with negligible number of IPOs. After the retreat following the 2008 cash related crisis, IPOs ground to a halt, and for specific years after, new postings were extraordinary. Even more starting late, a huge piece of the IPO buzz has moved to an accentuation on the alleged unicorns—new organizations that have landed at private valuations of more than $1 billion.

Financial specialists and the media intensely estimate on these organizations and their choice to open up to the world by means of an IPO or remain private.

Understanding an IPO

Before an IPO, an organization is viewed as private. As a privately owned business, the business has developed with a moderately modest number of investors including early speculators like the originators, family, and companions alongside expert financial specialists, for example, financial speculators or holy messenger speculators.

At the point when an organization arrives at a phase in its development procedure where it trusts it is full grown enough for the rigors of SEC guidelines alongside the advantages and duties to open investors it will start to publicize its enthusiasm for opening up to the world. Normally, this phase of development will happen when an organization has arrived at a private valuation of roughly $1 billion, otherwise called unicorn status. In any case, privately owned businesses at different valuations with solid basics and demonstrated productivity potential can likewise fit the bill for an IPO, contingent upon the market rivalry and their capacity to meet posting necessities.

An IPO is a major advance for an organization. It furnishes the organization with access to collecting a great deal of cash. This gives the organization a more prominent capacity to develop and grow. The expanded straightforwardness and offer posting validity can likewise be a factor in helping it acquire better terms when looking for obtained assets also.

First sale of Bear parts of an association are esteemed through underwriting due steadiness. Right when an association opens up to the world, the as of late had private offer ownership changes over to open ownership and the present private financial specialists' offers become worth the open exchanging cost. Offer supporting can similarly join uncommon game plans for private to open offer belonging. Generally, the advancement from private to open is a key time for private examiners to exchange out and win the benefits they were envisioning. Private speculators may grasp their ideas in the open market or sell a piece or all of them for augmentations.

Meanwhile, the open market opens up an enormous open entryway for some money related authorities to buy shares in the association and contribute subsidizing to an association's financial specialists' worth. The open involves any individual or institutional monetary master who is enthusiastic about placing assets into the association. As a rule, the amount of offers the association sells and the expense for which offers sell are the making factors for the association's new financial specialists' worth regard. Financial specialists' worth still addresses offers controlled by examiners when it is both private and open, anyway with an IPO the speculators' worth augmentations on a very basic level with cash from the fundamental issuance.

Greatest IPOs

- Alibaba Group (BABA) in 2014 raising $25 billion
- American Insurance Group (AIG) in 2006 raising $20.5 billion
- VISA (V) in 2008 raising $19.7 billion
- General Motors (GM) in 2010 raising $18.15 billion
- Facebook (FB) in 2012 raising $16.01 billion

Lenders and the IPO Process

An IPO totally involves two areas. One, the pre-advancing time of the promoting. Two, the primary clearance of Bear itself. Exactly when an association is excited about an IPO it will elevate to underwriters by mentioning private offers or it can in like manner possess an open articulation to make interest. The underwriters lead the IPO technique and are picked by the association. An association may pick one or a couple of agents to supervise different bits of the IPO technique agreeably. The lenders are related with each piece of the IPO due constancy, document course of action, recording, publicizing, and issuance.

Steps to an IPO fuse the going with:

1. Underwriters present suggestion and valuations discussing their organizations, the best sort of security to issue, offering esteem, proportion of

offers, and assessed time apportioning for the market promoting.

2. The association picks its underwriters and authoritatively agrees to ensuring terms through an embracing understanding.

3. IPO gatherings are confined including agents, legitimate counsels, guaranteed open clerks, and Securities and Trade Commission masters.

4. Information as for the association is amassed for required IPO documentation.
   a. The S-1 Registration Statement is the basic IPO recording report. It has two areas: the arrangement and subtly held account information. The S-1 joins basic information about the ordinary date of the account. It will be adjusted as often as possible all through the pre-IPO process. The included blueprint is in like manner refreshed interminably.

5. Marketing materials are made for pre-publicizing of the new Bear issuance.
   a. Underwriters and authorities promote the offer issuance to measure solicitation and set up a last offering expense. Underwriters can make revisions to their money related examination all through the advancing technique. This can consolidate changing the IPO cost or issuance date as they see fit.
   b. Associations figure out how to meet unequivocal open offer offering essentials. Associations must hold quick to both exchange posting essentials and SEC necessities for open associations.

1. Form an administering body.

2. Ensure systems for specifying auditable money related and accounting information each quarter.
3. The association gives its ideas on an IPO date.
   a. Capital from the basic issuance to financial specialists is gotten as cash and recorded as speculators' an incentive on the advantage report. Along these lines, the advantage report offer worth winds up subject to the association's financial specialists' worth per share valuation totally.
4. Some post-IPO courses of action may be built up.
   a. Underwriters may have a foreordained time apportioning to buy an additional proportion of offers after the principal clearance of Bear date.
   b. Certain theorists may be at risk to quiet periods.

A common hold is a kind of money related vehicle made up of a pool of money assembled from various examiners to place assets into insurances, for instance, Bears, protections, cash market instruments, and various assets. Normal resources are worked by master money directors, who allocate the save's favourable circumstances and attempt to convey capital increments or pay for the store's theorists. A typical store's portfolio is sorted out and kept up to match the endeavour targets communicated in its framework.

Regular backings give close to nothing or individual theorists access to expertly supervised course of action of esteems, bonds and various securities. Each financial specialist, along these lines, takes an intrigue generally in the increments or hardships of the store. Normal resources put assets into innumerable assurances, and execution is by and large pursued as the modification in the outright market top of the save—controlled by the collecting execution of the shrouded endeavours.

The Basics of a Mutual Fund

Regular backings pool money from the contributing open and use that money to buy various insurances, by and large Bears and securities. The estimation of the basic hold association depends upon the show of the assurances it buys. Thusly, when you buy a unit or part of a common save, you are acquiring the presentation of its portfolio or even more definitively, a bit of the portfolio's value. Placing assets into a bit of a typical store is one of a kind in connection to placing assets into parts of Bear. As opposed to Bear, normal store offers don't give its holders any just rights. A segment of a typical store addresses interests in a wide scope of Bears (or various insurances) as opposed to just one holding.

That is the explanation the expense of a typical store offer is insinuated as the net asset regard (NAV) per offer, once in a while imparted as NAVPS. A save's NAV is deduced by parcelling the outright estimation of the assurances in the portfolio by the total entirety of offers uncommon. Noteworthy offers are those held by all financial specialists, institutional examiners, and companions authorities or insiders. Regular save offers can commonly be procured or recouped as required at the store's present NAV, which—rather than a Bear expense—doesn't shift during business area hours, yet is settled toward the piece of the course of action day.

The typical basic save holds numerous different securities, which means shared store financial specialists increment huge widening requiring little to no effort. Consider a money related pro who buys simply Google Bear before the association has an awful quarter. He stands to lose a ton of huge worth since most of his dollars are joined to one association. On the other hand, another money related master may buy parts of a common hold that happens to have some Google Bear. Right when Google has a dreadful quarter, she just loses a division as much since Google is just a little bit of the save's portfolio.

KEY TAKEAWAYS

- A shared hold is a sort of adventure vehicle containing a game plan of Bears, bonds or various securities.
- Mutual resources give close to nothing or individual money related pros access to separated, expertly administered portfolios effortlessly.
- Mutual resources are apportioned into a couple of sorts of classes, addressing the sorts of assurances they put assets into, their endeavour objectives, and the sort of benefits they search for.
- Mutual resources charge yearly costs (called cost extents) and, from time to time, commissions, which can impact their general returns.
- The bigger piece of money in chief upheld retirement plans goes into basic resources.

How Mutual Funds Work

A common store is both an endeavour and a genuine association. This twofold nature may give off an impression of being anomalous, yet it is equivalent to how a bit of AAPL is a depiction of Apple, Inc. Exactly when a theorist buys Apple Bear, he is acquiring part duty regarding association and its focal points. Basically, a mutual store money related expert is buying part duty regarding basic save association and its advantages. What makes a difference is that Apple is in the matter of making phones and tablets, while a mutual hold association is in the matter of making hypotheses.

Money related authorities typically increase an appearance from a common hold in three unique manners:

1. Income is earned from benefits on Bears and excitement on protections held in the store's portfolio. A store pays out about most of the compensation it gets during the time to fund owners as a scattering. Resources routinely give budgetary masters a choice either to get a check for appointments or to reinvest the salary and get more offers

2. If the store sells securities that have extended in esteem, the hold has a capital increment. Most resources furthermore pass on these increments to monetary masters in a dissemination.

3. If store assets increase in cost at this point are not sold by the hold boss, the save's offers increase in cost. You would then have the option to sell your normal save shares for an advantage in the market.

In case a typical hold is comprehended as a virtual association, its CEO is the store chairman, a portion of the time called its endeavour advisor. The hold boss is enrolled by an overseeing body and is legitimately dedicated to work to the best favourable position of basic store financial specialists. Most store boss are furthermore owners of the hold. There are very few unique delegates in a typical save association. The endeavour specialist or hold overseer may use a couple of specialists to help pick hypotheses or perform measurable studying. A hold clerk is kept on staff to figure the store's NAV, the step by step estimation of the portfolio that chooses whether offer expenses go up or down.

Most shared resources are a bit of a much greater hypothesis association; the best have a few distinctive basic resources. A segment of these store associations are names conspicuous to the general populace, for instance,

Sorts of Mutual Funds

Regular resources are isolated into a couple of sorts of groupings, addressing the sorts of assurances they have cantered for their portfolios and the sort of benefits they search for. There is a save for pretty much every kind of money related authority or hypothesis approach. Other ordinary sorts of basic resources join money market holds, section saves, elective resources, insightful beta resources, cut-off time saves, and even resources of-advantages, or shared sponsors that buy segments of other shared resources.

Worth Funds

The greatest class is that of significant worth or Bear resources. As the name proposes, this sort of store puts primarily in Bears. Inside this social occasion is distinctive sub-characterizations. Some worth resources are named for the size of the associations they put assets into little , mid-or huge top. Others are named by their endeavour approach: compelling improvement, pay orchestrated, worth, and others. Worth resources are similarly grouped by whether they put assets into family (U.S.) Bears or remote qualities. There are such countless different sorts of significant worth saves in light of the way that there are a wide scope of sorts of esteems. An exceptional strategy to appreciate the universe of significant worth resources is to use a style box, an instance of which is underneath.

CHAPTER FOUR

The Examples of Bear market Investment

Fixed-Income Funds

Another huge social occasion is the fixed compensation class. A fixed compensation shared store bases on adventures that pay a set tone of return, for instance, government protections, corporate protections, or other commitment instruments. The idea is that the save portfolio produces interest compensation, which by then passes on to speculators.

To a great extent suggested as security saves, these advantages are normally adequately supervised and hope to buy modestly thought little of protections in order to sell them at an advantage. These basic resources are likely going to pay more significant yields than presentations of store and cash publicize hypotheses, yet security accounts aren't without peril. Since there are a wide scope of sorts of protections, security resources can move altogether depending upon where they contribute. For example, a store increasing down to earth involvement in exceptional yield trash protections is much more risky than a save that places assets into government securities. In addition, pretty much all security resources are subject to advance expense possibility, which suggests that if rates go up the estimation of the hold goes down.

Record Funds

Another social occasion, which has ended up being extraordinarily standard over the latest couple of years, falls under the moniker "record holds." Their endeavour framework relies upon the conviction that it is hard, and normally expensive, to endeavour to beat the market dependably.

Balanced Funds

Balanced resources put assets into the two Bears and bonds to lessen the risk of prologue to some favourable position class. Another name for this sort of normal hold is "asset assignment support." A theorist may plan to find the task of these advantages among asset classes decently consistent, anyway it will differ among resources. This present hold's goal is asset appreciation with lower possibility. In any case, these advantages pass on a comparative peril and can be as liable to change as various requests of benefits.

A near sort of save is known as a favourable position appropriation money. Targets resemble those of a sensible store, anyway these sorts of benefits typically don't have to hold a foreordained degree of any favourable position class. The portfolio head is as such offered chance to switch the extent of bit of leeway classes as the economy goes through the business cycle.

Money Market Funds

The money market contains safe (chance free) transient commitment instruments, for the most part government

Treasury bills. This is a protected spot to stop your money. You won't get extensive returns, yet you won't have to worry over losing your head. A regular return is fairly more than the aggregate you would pick up in a customary checking or financial balance and to some degree not exactly the ordinary validation of store (CD). While money advertise resources put assets into ultra-safe assets, during the 2008 budgetary crisis, some cash showcase resources experienced hardships after the offer expense of these benefits, ordinarily pegged at $1, fell underneath that level and broke the buck.

Pay Funds

Pay resources are named for their inspiration: to give current compensation on a suffering reason. These advantages put chiefly in government and high gauge corporate commitment, holding these protections until improvement in order to give interest streams. While finance property may recognize in worth, the basic objective of these advantages is to give suffering salary to budgetary masters. In this manner, the group for these advantages includes preservationist theorists and retirees. Since they produce ordinary pay, charge discerning theorists may need to avoid these benefits.

Around the world/International Funds

An overall hold (or remote store) places just in assets arranged outside your country of source. Overall resources, then, can contribute wherever around the world, including inside your country of birthplace. It's hard to orchestrate these benefits as either more risky or more secure than family adventures, yet they have would when all is said in done be dynamically capricious and have an extraordinary country and political perils. On the opposite side, they can, as a significant part of a composed portfolio, truly lessening possibility by extending diversification since the benefits in outside countries may be uncorrelated with returns at home. Regardless of the way that the world's economies are winding up dynamically interrelated, everything considered, another economy some spot is outmanoeuvring the economy of your country of beginning.

Distinguishing strength Funds

This gathering of regular resources is a more noteworthy measure of a far reaching order that contains resources that have exhibited to be unmistakable yet don't generally have a spot with the more unyielding characterizations we've delineated as of not long ago. These sorts of basic resources repudiate broad improvement to concentrate on a particular section of the economy or a concentrated on strategy. Territory resources are cantered around method resources went for unequivocal divisions of the economy, for instance, cash related, development, prosperity, and so on. Region resources can, thusly, be inconceivably flighty since the Bears in a given part will as a rule be significantly connected with each other. There is a progressively significant likelihood for colossal increments, yet moreover a section may succumb to (occurrence the cash related territory in 2008 and 2009).

Nearby supports make it less complex to focus on a specific geographic area of the world. This can mean focusing on an increasingly broad locale (state Latin America) or an individual country (for example, just Brazil). A touch of breathing space of these advantages is that they make it more straightforward to buy Bear in remote countries, which can for the most part be problematic and expensive. Much equivalent to for division saves, you have to recognize the high risk of adversity, which occurs if the territory goes into a dreadful subsidence.

Socially-careful resources (or good resources) put extraordinarily in associations that meet the criteria of explicit standards or feelings. For example, some socially careful resources don't place assets into "offense" endeavours, for instance, tobacco, blended beverages, weapons or nuclear power. The idea is to get forceful execution while up 'til now keeping up a strong still, little voice. Other such resources put basically in green advancement, for instance, sun situated and wind control or reusing.

Exchange Traded Funds (ETFs)

A reshape on the regular save is the exchange exchanged store (ETF). These constantly pervasive endeavour vehicles pool theories and use techniques dependable with regular resources, anyway they are sorted out as theory accepts that are exchanged on Bear exchanges and have the extra focal points of the features of Bears. For example, ETFs can be obtained and sold whenever all through the exchanging day. ETFs can moreover be undermines or acquired nervous. ETFs moreover usually pass on lower costs than the equivalent regular save. Various ETFs in like manner advantage from dynamic options markets where budgetary experts can support or utilize their positions. ETFs in like manner acknowledge evaluation focal points from shared resources. The notoriety of ETFs tends to their adaptability and solace.

Focal points of Mutual Funds

There is an arrangement of reasons that basic resources have been the retail theorist's vehicle of choice for a significant long time. The mind bigger piece of money in supervisor upheld retirement plans goes into shared resources.

Upgrade

Upgrade, or the mixing of adventures and assets inside a portfolio to diminish danger, is one of the upsides of placing assets into basic resources. Masters advocate improvement as a strategy for improving portfolio return while diminishing its peril. Obtaining singular association Bears and offsetting them with present day fragment Bears, for example, offers some upgrade. Nevertheless, a truly expanded portfolio has assurances with different capitalizations and adventures and bonds with moving improvements and sponsor. Acquiring a typical hold can achieve improvement more affordable and snappier than by buying solitary securities. Tremendous basic sponsors commonly guarantee a few particular Bears in a wide scope of undertakings. It wouldn't be rational for a monetary authority to develop this kind of a portfolio with a humble amount of money.

Simple Access

Market on the significant Bear trades, shared assets can be purchased and sold without breaking a sweat, making them profoundly fluid speculations. Likewise, with regards to specific kinds of benefits, as remote values or fascinating items, common assets are frequently the most doable way—indeed, some of the time the main way—for individual financial specialists to take part.

Economies of Scale

Shared assets likewise give economies of scale. Getting one extras the speculator of the various commission charges expected to make an expanded portfolio.

Purchasing just a single security at a time prompts huge trade charges, which will gobble up a decent piece of the speculation. Likewise, the $100 to $200 an individual speculator may have the option to manage the cost of is normally insufficient to purchase a round part of the Bear, yet it will buy numerous common reserve shares. The littler divisions of shared assets enable financial specialists to exploit dollar cost averaging.

Proficient Management

An essential bit of leeway of shared assets isn't picking Bears and oversee speculations. Rather, an expert venture chief deals with the majority of this utilizing cautious research and apt trading. Financial specialists buy reserves since they frequently don't have opportunity or the skill to deal with their very own portfolios, or they don't approach a similar sort of data that an expert store has. A shared reserve is a moderately cheap path for a little speculator to get a full-time supervisor to make and screen ventures. Most private, non-institutional cash directors manage high-total assets people—individuals with at any rate six figures to contribute. Notwithstanding, shared assets, as noted above, require much lower speculation essentials. In this way, these assets give a minimal effort approach to singular financial specialists to experience and ideally advantage from expert cash the board.

Economies of Scale

Since a shared reserve purchases and sells a lot of protections one after another, its trade expenses are lower than what an individual would pay for.

A market solicitation is a buy or offer solicitation to be executed immediately at the present market costs. For whatever period of time that there are willing vendors and buyers, publicize solicitations are filled. Market solicitations are used when conviction of execution is a need over the expense of execution. A market solicitation is the least troublesome of the solicitation types.

Sorts OF ORDERS

The most outstanding sorts of solicitations are market orders, limit demands, and stop-setback orders.

- A market solicitation is a solicitation to buy or sell a security immediately. This sort of solicitation guarantees that the solicitation will be executed, yet doesn't guarantee the execution cost. A market demand generally will execute at or near the present offer (for a sell demand) or ask (for a buy demand) cost. In any case, it is noteworthy for theorists to recall that the last-exchanged cost isn't generally the expense at which a market solicitation will be executed.
- A cut-off solicitation is a solicitation to buy or sell a security at a specific expense or better. A buy most remote point solicitation must be executed at the limit cost or lower, and a sell cut-off solicitation must be executed at the most extreme expense or higher. Model: An examiner needs to purchase bits of ABC Bear for near $10. The budgetary master could show a cut-off demand for this aggregate and this solicitation will conceivably execute if the expense of ABC Bear is $10 or lower.
- A stop demand, in like manner implied as a stop-hardship solicitation is a solicitation to buy or sell a Bear once the expense of the Bear lands at the foreordained cost, known as the stop cost. Right

when the stop cost is reached, a stop solicitation transforms into a market demand.
- A buy stop solicitation is entered at a stop cost over the present market cost. Monetary masters all things considered use a buy stop solicitation to limit an adversity or secure an advantage on a Bear that they have undermines. A sell stop solicitation is entered at a stop cost underneath the present market cost. Money related authorities all things considered use a sell stop solicitation to limit a setback or secure an advantage on a Bear they guarantee.

Market Order versus Point of imprisonment Order: An Overview

Exactly when a money related expert places in a solicitation to buy or sell a Bear, there are two head execution decisions: put in the solicitation "at advertise" or "at cut-off." Market solicitations are exchanges expected to execute as quick as possible at the present or market cost. On the other hand, a point of restriction solicitation sets the most outrageous or least cost at which you are anxious to buy or sell.

Acquiring Bear is to some degree like buying a vehicle. With a vehicle, you can pay the dealer's sticker cost and get the vehicle. Or then again you can organize an expense and decay to complete the plan with the exception of if the vender meets your expense. The money related exchange works moreover.

A market requesting manages the execution of the sales; the cost of the security is associate to the speed of finishing the trade. Most far off point sales manage the cost; if the security's worth is beginning at now resting outside of the parameters set in the most outrageous requesting, the trade doesn't happen.

- A showcase requesting relies upon finishing a sales at the speediest speed.
- A most outrageous sales is worried over guaranteeing that value musings are met before a trade is executed.
- Market requesting offer an undeniably basic probability that a sales will inclusion, at any rate there are no affirmations, as sales are in danger to accessibility.

Market Orders

Right when the layman envisions a normal budgetary trade, he considers market orders. These sales are the most chief purchase and sell trades; an agent gets a security trade request, and that sales is set up at the present market cost.

Regardless of the manner in which that market requesting offer a continuously obvious probability of a trade being executed, there is no certification that the trade will genuinely association. All cash related trade trades are in danger to the accessibility of given Bears and can move essentially dependent on the masterminding, the size of the requesting, and the liquidity of the Bear.

All sales are set up inside present need rules. At whatever point a market sales is set, there is dependably the risk of market changes happening between the time the master gets the sales and the time the trade is executed. This is particularly a worry for more noteworthy requesting, which put aside more exertion to fill and, if colossal enough, can really move the market with no other person. From time to time the market of individual Bears might be ended or suspended.

A market request that is set in the wake of market hours will be filled at the market cost on open the going with market day.

For instance, a cash related expert enters a requesting to buy 100 pieces of an affiliation XYZ Inc. at market cost. Since the money related master picks whatever value XYZ offers are going for, his trade will be filled rather rapidly—at, state, $87.50 per share.

There are two basic sorts of Bears: principal Bear and bolstered Bear.

Standard Bear

Standard Bear is, well, common. Precisely when individuals talk about Bears everything considered they are no vulnerability recommending this sort. Truly, most of Bear gave is in this structure. We in a general sense went over highlights of regular Bear in the last segment. Ordinary offers address possession in an affiliation and a case (benefits) on a section of focal points. Analysts get one ruling for every plan to pick the board individuals, who manage the certifiable choices made by the authorities.

Over the long haul, ordinary Bear, by strategies for capital headway, yields more noteworthy yields than fundamentally every other undertaking. This better yield consolidates some huge disadvantages since standard Bears incorporate the most hazard. In the event that an affiliation crashes and burns and sells, the basic budgetary authorities won't get cash until the advance pros, bondholders, and favoured examiners are paid.

Favoured Bear

Favoured Bear converses with some degree proprietorship in an affiliation in any case generally doesn't go with a tantamount greater part guideline rights. (This may shift subordinate upon the relationship.) With favoured offers analysts are consistently ensured a fixed advantage until the end of time. This isn't proportionate to fundamental Bear, which has variable advantages that are never ensured. Another bit of room is that if there ought to be an event of liquidation favoured theorists are satisfied before the commonplace money related master (yet after duty holders). Favoured Bear may in like way be callable, recommending that the affiliation has the choice to buy the thoughts from money related pros at whatever point in any way at all (when in doubt for a premium).

A couple of individuals consider favoured Bear to be more like commitment than esteem. A not too bad strategy to consider these sorts of offers is to believe them to be in securities and ordinary offers. (If you don't grasp bonds guarantee moreover to take a gander at our bond instructional exercise.)

Different Classes of Bear

Typical and favoured are the two rule kinds of Bear; nevertheless, it's moreover functional for associations to modify different classes of Bear in any way they need. The most broadly perceived reason behind this is the association requiring the just ability to remain with a particular social occasion; hence, different classes of offers are given unmistakable popularity based rights. For example, one class of offers would be held by a select social event who are given ten decisions in favour of each offer while a beneath normal would be given to the vast majority of theorists who are given one decision in favour of each offer.

At the point when there is more than one class of Bear, the classes are generally assigned as Class An and Class B. Berkshire Hathaway (ticker: BRK), the organization of Warren Buffett (probably the best financial specialist ever), has two classes of Bear. The various structures are spoken to by setting the letter behind the ticker image in a structure this way: "BRKa, BRKb" or "BRK.A, BRK.B".

Step by step instructions to Pick Bears: 7 Things You Should Know

Do schoolwork before purchasing shares.

Not all speculators are huge into Bear picking. Numerous portfolios incorporate a couple of Bears that the financial specialist thinks have potential (and that pay profits). When you choose to take a stab at Bear picking, it's critical to get your work done. You need a decent esteem – particularly on the off chance that you intend to clutch something for some time.

Profit development

Search for patterns in an organization's profit development. After some time, do the profit for the most part increment? Assuming this is the case, it's a quite decent sign that the organization is accomplishing something right. You don't have to see a sensational increment for an organization to be a decent decision, however. Indeed, even little, ordinary improvement over an extensive stretch of time can be a positive pointer.

Steadiness

The idea of the securities trade – at any rate everyday and year-to-year – is instability. Sooner or later, an organization will lose an incentive in the business sectors. In any case, the main thing is long haul steadiness. By and large, pattern lines smooth out and head higher. Search for that with individual organizations also. An organization that climates the downturns and returns moderately solid, and that possibly appears to have genuine issue when every other person does, is presumably a decent wagered.

Relative quality in industry

Start by looking industry addressed in the market. Does it have future potential? Industry can be a mind blowing screener while contributing. Regardless, when picking individual Bears in an industry, for instance, imperativeness, you need to look at where the association fits in. Is it well-set against contenders? Is there a touch of slack that empowers it to stand out? Given this is valid, you may have found a victor.

Commitment worth extent

All associations pass on commitment – even Amazon.com (ticker: AMZN) and Apple (AAPL). In any case, that doesn't mean you can't use that commitment as a marker while contributing. Watch out for associations with high commitment levels in regard to their worth. To find this number, confine the total liabilities on the association bookkeeping report by the total entirety of financial specialist esteem. For those with a lower risk versatility, that number should be at 0.3 or less. There are exclusions. For example, look at the commitment worth extent over an industry. In the improvement business, with its reliance on commitment sponsoring, a higher extent might be commendable. Just guarantee your pick is as per industry measures.

Worth benefit extent

You've likely watched this around. The P/E extent offers an extent of how well a Bear's expense is doing in regard to the association's pay. When using basic assessment and worth contributing methods, P/E extent is seen as an essential marker. To find the P/E extent, parcel the present offer expense by its benefit per share. If an association is exchanging at $40 per share, and the salary per offer are $2.50, the P/E extent is 16. The higher the P/E extent, the more likely it is that there will be important advancement later on. P/E extent isn't everything while contributing, yet it might be helpful to consider associations in a comparable industry or part.

The administrators

What sum do you trust in the people at the most noteworthy purpose of an association? Does their drive advance an unfaltering and trustworthy association culture? Is the association innovative? Flexible? How are they putting over into the association and in the system? A well-regulated association is normally one that acknowledges Bear costs that example higher. Consider shock too. An association with flexibility can atmosphere transient shames – especially if an organization change prompts forward power. It's hard to gauge the consequence of a shame, anyway obtaining during a dive can accumulate you a nice course of action and position your contributing portfolio for future accomplishment.

Benefits

Various theorists like to look at benefits when picking individual Bears. An association that pays benefits is normally one with a degree of sufficiency – especially if it's a benefit nobility that is extended its payout dependably consistently for an impressive period of time. Watch out for associations that have incredibly extraordinary returns, in any case. A spike in benefit yield can mean an association is getting rushed. High benefits can in like manner at times be an indication that an association isn't placing enough in itself. Quest for associations that pay unassuming, yet ordinary (and growing) benefits after some time.

Record keeping and evaluations

A Bear record is an ordered posting of securities held by a business firm in light of a legitimate concern for customers. The Bear record demonstrates the names of the veritable and important owners, aggregates and territories of all insurances held by the firm. The record must be invigorated at whatever point an exchange is executed.

Checking your Bear

A yearly Bear take is an essential bit of Bear control and is the best way to deal with screen your Bear. You should similarly execute an advancing structure for following things you have acquired and sold.

A practical system for following your Bear will empower you to work out when to reorder Bear.

Bear taking

Playing out a Bear take incorporates making a once-over, or Bear, of all the Bear you hold. You should have the alternative to pursue everything in your Bear by its:

- unique thing number
- stored territory
- selling cost

- Bear number
- cost
- quantity
- source of reserve
- applicable cost
- point-of-offer nuances.

Bear taking is a gainful exercise that can empower you to recognize lost, taken or hurt things. You may have the alternative to limit these things as an adversity, on occasion against the cost of items sold, for accounting purposes.

Dependent upon your Bear and the size of your business, you may be legally dedicated to play out a yearly Bear take. Get acquainted with your legitimate duties for Bear taking.

Bear taking results should be consolidated into your record keeping.

Manual Bear organization

Manual Bear organization best suits associations that pass on a humble amount of Bear. A manual Bear organization system may include:

- a Bear book to record the things you have acquired and sold
- a reorder system reliant on your Bear book
- labels or codes for everything in your Bear, including information about the estimation of everything, when you got it and its territory.

PC based Bear organization

You can use essential PC based ventures to manage your Bear. PC tasks can pursue what Bear you solicitation and sell, and record the costs. The program may in like manner join a scanner and motivation behind offer (POS) machine. Various greater freight associations in like manner offer sweeping on the web systems to pursue shipments.

Bear control tasks can give information on explicit Bear organization techniques, similarly as help on express Bear organization issues. You may in like manner have the alternative to find a program that is unequivocal to your industry or the kind of Bear you hold.

In case you play the money related exchange (in the event that you're never again shell shocked by the insecurity of the ongoing years) you may need to know a little about the taxability of your insurances exchanges.

Capital Gains Tax

Any advantage you acknowledge from the leeway of a Bear held for at any rate a whole year is outfitted at the whole deal capital increments rate, which is lower than the rate associated with your other assessable compensation. It's 15% if you are in a 25% or higher cost area and only 5% if you are in the 15% or lower obligation segment. Advantages from Bears held for not actually a year are outfitted at your normal individual obligation rate.

Customary profits earned on your Bear property are exhausted at standard annual assessment rates, not at capital additions rates. In any case, "qualified profits" are saddled at an exceptionally invaluable capital increases pace of 0% to a limit of 15%. For profits to be named "qualified" they should be paid by a U.S. partnership or a certified remote organization and the holding time of the Bear must be over 60 days. There are a lot of different special cases and definitions, so check with your merchant or duty consultant to check whether the profits for your Bear property are "qualified." Dividends on Bear held in a certified retirement plan are not assessable pay.

Bear Sales

When deciding your benefit from a Bear deal, it's essential to comprehend the equation, however the importance of the factors in the recipe. Certain conditions connected to the factors can lessen your duty risk when you sell. Numerous citizens accept they should make good on government obligations on everything of the check they get from the deal - false. You can subtract your premise.

The recipe is: Sales Proceeds − Basis = Taxable Profit or Deductible Loss

Deal continues can be decreased by commissions paid to the agent.

The Wash Rule

Numerous financial specialists profit by selling a Bear in a losing position to balance an increase, at that point pivot and repurchase the Bear right.

Be that as it may, the IRS won't enable a speculator to guarantee a capital misfortune on the off chance that you sell a Bear and repurchase it inside 30 days. The "wash rule" keeps you from asserting a misfortune on a closeout of Bear on the off chance that you purchase substitution Bear inside the 30 days prior or after the deal and you will lose the counterbalance.

Capital Losses

One of the huge constraints in Bear contributing is the measure of misfortunes you are permitted to deduct on your expense form. On the off chance that you sell Bears at a misfortune, you may deduct just $3,000 every year; the rest of the misfortune is conveyed forward to future years. You may apply capital misfortunes against capital gains in the present and future years to net out the general benefit or shortfall.

Deductible Investment Expenses

A duty derivation regularly ignored by financial specialists is the expense of the executives charges paid to dealers, more often than not for the board of common store accounts or for warning administrations. You may deduct these charges as a venture cost on Schedule An of your government form. Some business 1099s or year-end explanations will express the aggregate for the year, yet many don't. You may need to get your agent to discover the amount you paid.

CHAPTER FIVE

Where to Buy and Sell Bear Market Investment

Tips

- Decide whether to experience an online business firm or through an eye to eye representative.
- After assessing a Bear, choose the costs you'd like to buy at, so you realize whether to make a "market" or "restricted" request.
- To save money on intermediary charges, you can get a few Bears legitimately from the organization.

Financial specialists most usually purchase and trade Bear through representatives.

You can set up a record by keeping money or Bears in an investment fund. Firms like Charles Schwab and Citigroup's Smith Barney unit offer investment funds that can be overseen on the web or with a representative face to face. On the off chance that you incline toward purchasing and selling Bears on the web, you can utilize destinations like E-Trade or Ameritrade. Those are only two of the most outstanding electronic businesses, however numerous huge firms have online choices also.

When you open a record you will tell your intermediary what number of and what kinds of Bears you'd like to buy. The specialist executes the trade for the your benefit. Thusly, the person in question acquires a commission, ordinarily a few pennies for every offer. Internet market destinations normally charge lower commission expenses, in light of the fact that a large portion of the markets done electronically.

In the wake of choosing the Bears that you need to buy, you can either make an "advertise request" or a "limit request." A market request is one in which you demand a Bear buy at the overall market cost. An utmost request is the point at which you solicitation to purchase a Bear at a restricted cost. For example, on the off chance that you need to purchase Bear in Dell at $60 an offer, and the Bear is presently market at $70, at that point the merchant would hold on to secure the offers until the value meets your utmost.

While acquiring Bears through an agent has its focal points, there are different approaches to purchase Bear. You can buy Bears straightforwardly through the organization. Locales like DRIPInvestor.com will demonstrate a rundown of organizations that permit direct-purchase of Bears.

The least demanding and least expensive approach to purchase offers is online based on what's known as a 'share managing stage'. These stages enable you to purchase shares from any organization recorded on the Bear trade and different abroad trades.

There's the fundamental Bear trade – the London Bear Trade, where you get an entire host of organizations including the huge players, for example, Marks and Spencer. At that point there's the Alternative Investment Market (AIM), which records littler creating organizations that you might not have known about.

Organizations get recorded on the Bear trade after they have finished an Initial Public Offering, a procedure which essentially takes the organization from being private to open – enabling others to in the end purchase partakes in it.

You'll generally have the option to purchase and sell offers market on the securities trade. In any case, the cost is dictated by the free market activity from planned purchasers and venders at a specific time – extreme interest will drive up the expense (while low request will do the inverse).

Regardless of whether you know the careful offer you need to purchase, despite everything you'll need to set up an market record and ensure there is sufficient cash in it before you can purchase the offer.

When you've done this, you can sign into your record and quest for the offer you need to purchase. You can either purchase an amount of offers, or a worth – whichever you pick, you need enough cash in your managing record to cover both this and any managing charges.

When you've chosen how you need to trade a cost will be cited, when you've acknowledged the value the offers will at that point appear in your portfolio.

The most effective method to sell shares

Selling offers is similarly as simple as getting them. Every stage's site will work marginally in an unexpected way, yet the guideline is the equivalent for each.

On the off chance that you have set up a chosen one record (as clarified above), as you don't hold the offer authentications, you need to sell the offers through the stage you got them from.

When you sell your offers you'll have two choices, you can either:

1. Sell your offers by number, or
2. Sell your offers by their worth

Just in case if the event that you need to sell the full holding (i.e., every one of the offers you have in that organization), you'll need to choose number of offers.

At the point when you place the game plan you will be shown a referred to cost for the freedom of the offers. You customarily have an obliged time allotment to pick (e.g., 15 seconds), and the worth referred to won't generally be as high as the worth you got them for. If you recognize, by then any money you have created utilizing the arrangement will show up in the record.

Pointers to look before contributing

If you put assets into Bears, by then I figure you should not focus on markers more, you ought to just to make a fundamental assessment of that particular Bear you have to contribute. It is a good Bears if all of the criteria matches like the P/E extent, benefit, Rate of improvement, Stake holding rate, etc.

In case you have to use any kind of marker, by then you may use moving typical. Markers are just established on intraday exchanging .

Really, it's outlandish that you'll find a Bear with every one of the ten trademarks, yet a Bear with even half of them is a super-solid choice. Get a Bear with anyway numerous trademarks as would be judicious and you likely have a champ.

The association has rising advantages

The very exemplification of a compelling association is its ability to make an advantage. In all honesty, advantage is without a doubt the most critical budgetary part of an association. Without advantage, an association leaves business. In case a business closes its passages, private vocations vanish. In this manner, charges don't get paid. This infers the lawmaking body can't limit and pay its workers and the people who are liable to open assistance.

The association has rising arrangements

Looking total ideas of an association is suggested as researching the top-line numbers.

An association (or agents) can mess around with various numbers on a compensation enunciation; there are twelve particular ways to deal with look at pay. Salary are the pith of an association, anyway the top line gives you an undeniable and clear number to look it. The outright arrangements (or gross arrangements or gross pay) number for an association is all the more eagerly to fudge.

The association has low liabilities

Considering, most money related masters would want to have an association with by and large low commitment than one with high commitment. A ton of commitment will kill a for the most part not too bad association.

Since an association with low commitment has getting power, it can misuse openings, for instance, expecting authority over an adversary or verifying an association that offers an extra advancement to help move present or future advantage improvement.

Notice that you aren't talking about an association with no commitment. An association with no commitment or little in the technique for liabilities is a solid association. In any case, in a circumstance where you can acquire at really low rates, it pays to expect some commitment and use it capably.

Besides, see that liabilities are an issue. It isn't continually customary commitment that may sink an association. Envision a situation where that association is essentially spending more money than it's getting. Liabilities or "hard and fast liabilities" considers everything that an association is resolved to pay, paying little heed to whether it's a whole deal bond (whole deal commitment), paying workers, or the water bill. Current expenses should be more than verified by current compensation, yet you would lean toward not to hoard whole deal commitment, which means a channel on future compensation.

The Bear is at an arrangement cost

You can look at the estimation of an association in a couple of various ways, yet the primary concern you should look at is the expense to-pay extent (P/E extent). It attempts to interface the expense of the association's Bear to the association's net advantages referred to on a for each offer reason. For example, if an association has an expense of $15 per share and the pay are $1 per share, by then the P/E extent is 15.

Benefits are creating

Benefits are the whole deal examiner's nearest partner. Wouldn't it be inconceivable if following several extensive stretches of owning that Bear, you got outright benefits that truly eclipsed what your special theory was? That is more run of the mill than you know!

Benefit advancement furthermore passes on with it the potential improvement of the Bear itself. A dependably rising benefit is a positive sign at the Bear expense. The contributing open sees that a creating benefit is an astounding and indisputable sign of the association's present and future financial prosperity.

An association may have the alternative to fudge salary and other sensitive or flexible figures, yet when a benefit is paid, that is hard check that the association is winning with its net advantage. Given that, just overview the whole deal Bear diagram (say five years or a greater amount of) an anticipated benefit paying association, and on various occasions out of 100, that Bear expense is befuddling upward in a similar model.

The market is creating

Explore economics and publicize data and use this information to further channel your contributing choices. You could run a phenomenal association, yet if your fortunes are made when a million people buy from you, and one year from now that number advisors to 800,000, and the year after that it contracts again, what will happen to your fortunes?

The association is in a field with a high block to entry

A high block to entry basically infers that associations that battle with you will have a serious time overcoming your favoured position. This empowers you to create and leave your resistance in the build-up.

The association has a low political profile

History exhibits that associations that are politically centred around either authentically or by relationship (by being in a loathed industry) can persevere. There was a period that holding tobacco associations in your portfolio was what could be contrasted with garlic to a vampire.

Considering, you may need to hold a Bear in a conspicuous industry or an unremarkable industry rather than one that attracts undue (negative) thought.

The Bear is optionable

An optionable Bear (which has call and put choices available on it) infers that you have added ways to deal with profit by it (or the ability to constrain potential incidents). Decisions give a financial specialist ways to deal with overhaul gains or yield included salary.

How about we expect you do in assurance find the perfect Bear, and you truly weight up and buy indistinguishable number of offers from you can lay your hands on, yet you don't have any more money to buy another bunch of offers.

Fortunately, you see that the Bear is optionable and see that you can assess by obtaining a consider decision that empowers you to be bullish on 100 ideas with a modest quantity of the cash expected to truly buy 100 offers. As the Bear takes off, you're prepared to take benefits by getting the cash for out the think about decision without reaching the Bear circumstance using any and all means.

By and by, with your Bear at nosebleed levels, you're getting a little on edge that this Bear is maybe at an unsustainable level, so you get some put choices to shield your concealed increases from your Bear. Right when your Bear encounters a correction, you cash out your put with an invaluable expansion. With the Bear down, you take the profits from your put option recognized gains and buy a more prominent measure of the Bear at positive expenses.

Portfolio improvement is the most central and convincing technique for constraining threats in the cash related markets. Upgrade is the specialty of spreading ones capital by placing assets into different insurances, as a strategy for ensuring prologue to one sort of advantage is compelled. The preparation goes far in diminishing the precariousness of your portfolio after some time.

An extended portfolio will reliably involve different sorts of cash related instruments tending to various endeavours or sections. While upgrade doesn't guarantee protection against threats, it goes far in promising one achieves cash related goals easily.

Portions of a Diversified Portfolio

Private Bears

Bears speak to the most gigantic chunk of most extended theory portfolios. It is in light of the fact that they offer opportunities to higher advancement over a broad stretch. In any case, transient examiners diminish their introduction to Bears, as they are ordinarily more unusual than various securities. While precariousness is something worth being grateful for, it can similarly kill you, especially amidst a downturn.

Bonds

Bonds are also an essential component of an expanded portfolio. For cash focused money related authorities then this is the best approach, given that protections give standard premium compensation. Protections moreover go about as a cushion against the issues that as often as possible shake the business parts.

Monetary pros focused on prosperity rather than improvement ought to find comfort in U.S Treasury or stunning protections. Astonishing bonds are ideal for budgetary authorities who are glad to battle with lower whole deal returns.

Transient Investments

Flashing adventures furthermore give an ideal technique for extending a hypothesis portfolio. Such adventures fuse money market saves, which are conventionalist hypotheses expected to offer security and straightforward access to money. Given that they are ideal for ensuring capital, they will as a rule give lower returns than security holds.

Verifications of Deposit anyway without the liquidity advertised

Part Funds

Part assets are protections that put resources into a wide cluster of Bears. Be that as it may, they centre around a specific fragment of the economy along these lines giving presentation to a different scope of offers in the given part. Area assets are perfect broadening resources as they enable financial specialists to appreciate openings in various periods of monetary cycles.

Item Funds

Experienced financial specialists numerous now and again include items in their venture portfolio by putting resources into product reserves. Such assets give presentation to things, for example, oil, gas among other normal assets traded the money related market. Such resources go about as a decent fence against expansion.

Land Funds

Generally alluded to as Real Estate Investment Trusts, REITs will in general grow a venture portfolio introduction into the land division. Such assets put exclusively in loads of organizations with activities in the land part. Such protections additionally give some degree of security against the danger of swelling.

Approaches To Diversify a speculation portfolio

Portfolio expansion has its interests and systems that fluctuate contingent upon one's speculation methodology. Spreading a venture portfolio among various speculation vehicles is a regularly utilized enhancement methodology

The methodology includes including money, Bears, securities, common assets just as ETFs in a venture crate. For this situation, one can focus on resources that have not moved a similar way to a similar degree. Such a play guarantees, that' at whatever point one resource is on a descending direction its misfortunes are balanced by resources on an upward direction.

The subsequent methodology includes remaining enhanced inside each kind of venture. A financial specialist, for this situation, can incorporate protections that shift by part, the industry just as a locale or market capitalization. The thought is to put resources into protections that contrast with regards to development measurements, salary produced or esteem.

Putting resources into protections that shift with regards to hazard is another viable venture expansion technique. Rather than concentrating on a given arrangement of values, for example, blue-chip Bears or retail Bears, one can go for Bears or protections with various paces of profits. Differing paces of profits guarantee that at whatever point one resource is on a downtrend those on an upturn balance its misfortunes.

Proficient financial specialists make critical profits for understanding the way that portfolio enhancement is certifiably not an onetime assignment. For this situation, they complete checkups and rebalancing every once in a while. The rebalancing demonstration guarantees that the hazard a venture portfolio conveys is steady with monetary objectives and technique.

Speculation Portfolio Diversification Tips

Regardless of how energizing and luring protections look, never put all your cash in one Bear or one segment. The fundamental guideline of broadening is spreading money to a variety of protections. Endeavor to make a virtual shared store by putting resources into a bunch of Bears, bonds, metals, ETFs and so forth.

Put resources into Index or security assets, notwithstanding putting resources into Bears, monetary standards just as metals. The thing with putting resources into protections that track different records is that they give more prominent enhancement. Such records comprise of Bears from various divisions valuable for spreading one's presentation.

Putting resources into fixed pay arrangements likewise goes far in supporting one's portfolio against market unpredictability just as vulnerability. The procedure goes far in decreasing one's dangers just as misfortunes if there should be an occurrence of a downturn.

Develop Your Portfolio

Including speculations to a portfolio a normal premise ought to consistently enhance any broadening system. While utilizing the dollar cost averaging procedure, you can put cash all the time into different protections as a component of the technique

While differentiating a portfolio, it is additionally critical to realize when to get out. Proficient financial specialists remain current with their speculations and remain side by side with changes that make the business sectors move. For this situation, modifications should consistently become possibly the most important factor to trim where fundamental and include where required too

Advantages of Investment Portfolio Diversification

The essential objective of enhancement isn't simply to help execution yet to give the possibility to produce critical returns at a given degree of hazard.

Hazard the executives is one of the characteristics and advantages that accompany portfolio enhancement. Broadening brings down the unpredictability of a portfolio as not all advantages move a similar way. Putting resources into an assortment of non-associated resources likewise disposes of unsystematic hazard.

Putting resources into an assortment of non-related resources can likewise decrease the quantity of misfortunes accumulated in a bear advertise. At whatever point one security in a portfolio is gathering misfortunes, at that point other non-associated resources collecting benefits would have the option to balance its misfortunes.

Appropriate broadening is a powerful method for accomplishing portfolio enhancement. Chiefs, for this situation, put resources into a higher number of hazard resources while turning away the probability of going for broke than arranged from one single resource.

Enhancement makes it a lot simpler to secure capital while assigning cash to various ventures. The venture system enables one to put resources into an assortment of advantages along these lines diminish the dangers included essentially.

Broadening empowers one's speculation portfolio to keep developing when markets are blasting and when there is a downturn. A financial specialist, for this situation, can accomplish positive returns in a single market contingent upon protections contributed, even as another market keeps on creating negative returns.

End

Enhancement offers a decent number of advantages to financial specialists who comprehend what they are doing. First of all, it is loath for hazard and works for reasonable speculators. In addition, it shields capital from wild swings of the market, perfect for accomplishing long haul development.

Be that as it may, broadening can't keep one from losing cash in the market. Rather, it just decreases the hazard introduction. With regards to portfolio expansion, a financial specialist ought to consistently remember the hazard they are set up to acknowledge on contributed capital.

CHAPTER SIX

The Common Mistakes Made by Beginners

You've most likely heard that putting cash in the securities trade is the most ideal approach to develop your riches over the long haul. However, that is possibly valid on the off chance that you evade botches—and shockingly, a significant number of your normal propensities can truly disable your capacity to get rich on the securities trade. For example, we're set up to tune in to the news, pursue the group, and keep running for wellbeing when peril is hatching—however those inclinations can transform the securities trade into a losing suggestion. Here are a portion of the little speculation botches you have to figure out how to avoid in the event that you need to profit from your ventures.

1. Market Too Much

The more you purchase and sell your speculations, the more noteworthy your possibility of losing money. In the event that you put $10,000 in the S&P 500 of every 1995 and remained contributed through 2014, you would've earned 9.85 percent yearly or $59,593. However, in the event that you missed the best ten days during that 19-year time frame your arrival would have tumbled to 6.1

percent. After nineteen years, your underlying $10,000 would be worth $30,803.

Timing the market is a losing recommendation, and even the best seldom win.

2. Overlooking Fees

Before surrendering one dollar to a monetary counsellor or venture finance, comprehend the expenses. Truly, every store has a venture the executives charge, which extends from 0.03 percent to over 1.0 percent.

The SEC.gov site clarifies the effect of higher expenses on your ventures, however here's a model: Assume that you're a moderate speculator and contribute your $100,000 legacy for a long time in assets that profits a normal of 4 percent yearly. Toward the part of the bargain years, the venture that charged a 1.0 percent expense would be worth $180,000. The venture that charged 0.25 percent would be worth $210,000. That is a $30,000 contrast between the high and low charge reserves.

Try not to wrongly pay high charges. You can get wide broadening from Schwab's S&P 500 Index Fund (SWPPX) for an absolute bottom 0.03 percent yearly administration expense.

3. Not Investing Enough in Your 401(k) to Snare the Employer Match

In the event that your boss matches a percent of your commitment into your 401(k) or 403(b), at that point you're discarding free cash on the off chance that you don't contribute. Numerous businesses coordinate your own retirement plan commitment dollar-for-dollar up to 5 percent. In case you're gaining $70,000 every year, not putting $3,500 in your own retirement record isn't just denying yourself of the opportunity to develop a powerful retirement account however you're telling your boss, "I needn't bother with your $3,500, why not keep it!"

4. Placing Investments in the Wrong Accounts

Expenses play into most money related choices, and it'll cost you to put your budgetary resources in an inappropriate record.

When you've maximized your 401(k) coordinate, it pays to be savvy about which speculations go where, as various ventures get exhausted in an unexpected way. In case you're searching for speculations to place in an assessable record, you should hope to Bears, low-turnover Bear common assets, and civil bonds that you hope to hold as long as possible. That is on the grounds that your Bear increases are saddled at the capital additions rates, for the most part lower than the common annual expense rates. Much of the time, you're best off setting bonds, exhausted as common salary, in assessment advantaged retirement accounts.

5. Attempting to Beat the Market

Try not to attempt to beat the market, since chances are that you won't. Pursuing charming energy venture methodologies aren't probably going to satisfy. In 2015, 66 percent of dynamic cash directors neglected to beat the market returns. On the off chance that you like those chances, think about that somewhere in the range of 2005 and 2015, 82 percent of dynamic reserve directors neglected to beat the profits of the S&P 500 market list.

Incredible speculators from Warren Buffett to John Bogle champion putting resources into low-charge, showcase coordinating file reserves. Furthermore, the authentic financial trade information backs up the proposal to put for the whole deal in list reserves.

To get wealthy in the market, pick a reasonable resource allotment, put resources into low expense file reserves, and keep away from these venture botches. You won't become a medium-term tycoon, however over the long haul, you'll be set up for money related achievement.

No Market Plan

Experienced dealers get into an trade with a well-characterized plan. They know their careful section and leave focuses, the measure of money to put resources into the trade and the most extreme misfortune they are eager to take.

Amateur merchants might not have an market plan place before they begin trading. Regardless of whether they have an arrangement, they might be progressively inclined to stray from the characterized arrangement than would prepared merchants. Beginner brokers may switch course inside and out. For instance, going short after at first purchasing protections in light of the fact that the offer cost is declining—just to wind up getting whipsawed.

Pursuing Performance

Numerous financial specialists or brokers will choose resource classes, techniques, chiefs, and funds based on a current solid exhibition. The inclination that "I'm passing up extraordinary returns" has presumably prompted more awful speculation choices than some other single factor.

If a specific resource class, methodology, or reserve has done good for few years, we know one thing with assurance: We ought to have contributed three or four years back. Presently, notwithstanding, the specific cycle that prompted this incredible presentation might close to its end. The savvy cash is moving out, and the moronic cash is pouring in.

Not Regaining Balance

Rebalancing is the way toward restoring your portfolio to its objective resource distribution as plot in your speculation plan. Rebalancing is troublesome in light of the fact that it might drive you to sell the advantage class that is performing great and purchase a greater amount of your most noticeably awful performing resource class. This contrarian activity is hard for some beginner financial specialists.

In any case, a portfolio permitted to float with market returns ensures that advantage classes will be overweighed at market crests and underweighted at market lows—a recipe for lacklustre showing. Rebalance religiously and receive the long haul benefits.

Overlooking Risk Aversion

Try not to dismiss your hazard resilience, or your ability to go out on a limb. A few speculators can't stomach unpredictability and the good and bad times related with the financial trade or increasingly theoretical trades. Different financial specialists may need secure, normal intrigue salary. These generally safe resilience financial specialists would be in an ideal situation putting resources into the blue-chip loads of built up firms and should avoid progressively unpredictable development and new businesses shares.

Keep in mind that any speculation return accompanies a hazard. The most minimal hazard speculation accessible is U.S. Treasury bonds, bills, and notes. From that point, different sorts of ventures climb in the hazard stepping stool, and will likewise offer bigger comes back to make up for the higher hazard attempted. On the off chance that a speculation offers alluring returns, likewise see its hazard profile and perceive how a lot of cash you could lose if things turn out badly. Never contribute beyond what you can stand to lose.

Overlooking Your Time Horizon

Try not to put without a period skyline as a top priority. Consider in the event that you will require the assets you are bolting up into a venture before entering the trade. Additionally, decide to what extent—the time skyline—you need to put something aside for your retirement, a down payment on a home, or a school training for your tyke.

In the event that you are intending to gather cash to purchase a house, that could be all the more a medium-term time period. In any case, on the off chance that you are contributing to back a small kid's school instruction, that is all the more a long haul speculation. In the event that you are putting something aside for retirement 30 years thus, what the financial trade does this year or next shouldn't be the greatest concern.

When you comprehend your frame of reference, you can discover ventures that match that profile.

Not Using Stop-Loss Orders

A major sign that you don't have an market plan isn't utilizing stop-misfortune orders. Stop requests come in a few assortments and can restrict misfortunes because of antagonistic development in a Bear or the market in general. These requests will execute consequently once edges you set are met.

Tight stop misfortunes by and large imply that misfortunes are topped before they become sizable. In any case, there is a hazard that a stop request on long positions might be executed at levels beneath those predetermined should the security all of a sudden hole lower—as happened to numerous speculators during the Flash Crash. Indeed, even in light of that idea, the advantages of stop arranges far exceed the danger of halting out at an impromptu cost.

A conclusion to this normal market mix-up is the point at which a merchant drops a stop request on a losing trade just before it very well may be activated in light of the fact that they accept that the value pattern will invert.

Allowing Losses To develop

One of the characterizing qualities of effective speculators and brokers is their capacity to assume a little misfortune rapidly if an trade isn't working out and proceed onward to the following trade thought. Fruitless merchants, then again, can wind up deadened if an trade conflicts with them. Instead of making speedy move to top a misfortune, they may clutch a losing position with the expectation that the trade will in the end work out.

Financial trade news and media

The adjustments in the media, news and news coverage industry have achieved tremendous changes to the monetary business. The news like profit reports, acquisitions, IPOs or market estimations when all is said in done are caught in portion of seconds and transferred over the world. News has discovered the ability to travel quick and the merchants have discovered the capacity to respond quick!

Expecting that business sectors perform better with more data, the securities trades ought to perform effectively with the heaps of news. This, in any case, isn't the situation. The business sectors, with over-burden of data, are as yet one-sided. The financial specialists don't respond a lot to the positive news and respond uncontrollably to the negative ones.

Another reason is that more news doesn't mean better news. The surge of news is a greater amount of clam or and has a ton of insignificant material. The media makes a great deal of news to get open considerations and in some cases the important news get covered up as a result of being less substantial, and the unimportant ones get featured. This makes wasteful aspects in the market an enormous degree.

The news media are in steady challenge to catch the open consideration they have to endure. Survival for them requires finding and characterizing intriguing news, concentrating consideration on news that has informal potential (to expand their crowd), and, at whatever point conceivable, characterizing a continuous story that urges their group of spectators to stay consistent clients.

In this procedure, the estimation of the news appears to get lost and it is just the 'fascinating' and 'breaking' part that gets consideration. This transforms reality and the image indicated may not be the right one. This influences the market in a negative manner.

The news media are normally pulled in to monetary markets, in light of the fact that, in any event, the business sectors give consistent news as day by day value changes. Nothing beats the financial trade for sheer recurrence of possibly intriguing news things.

The securities trade has star quality. The open thinks of it as the Big Casino, the market for real players, and accepts that on some random day it fills in as a gauge of the status of the country—impressions that the media can encourage and profit by. Budgetary news may have incredible human intrigue potential to the degree that it manages the creation or breaking of fortunes. What's more, the money related media can display their perpetual lead, the market's exhibition, as a progressing story—one that gets the most steadfast recurrent clients. The main other normal generator of news on a practically identical scale is games. It is no mishap that money related news and sports news together represent generally 50% of the article substance of numerous papers today.

Be that as it may, the inquiry is the manner by which the news gets depicted and introduced. The news media welcomes banters on specific issues to get consideration, in this way, making more disarrays in the psyches of the effectively confounded financial specialists.

There is no deficiency of media accounts that attempt to address our inquiries regarding the market today, yet there is a lack in these records of important certainties or thought about elucidations of them. Numerous news stories in actuality appear to have been composed under a due date to deliver something—anything—to oblige the numbers from the market. The average such story, in the wake of taking note of the exceptional positively trending business sector, centres around extremely short-run insights. It for the most part states which gatherings of Bears have risen more than others as of late. In spite of the fact that these Bears are depicted as pioneers, there is no rhyme or reason to imagine that their presentation has caused the positively trending business sector. The news story may discuss the "standard thing" factors behind monetary development, for example, the Internet blast, in sparkling terms and with at any rate a trace of energetic salutation to our ground-breaking financial motor. The article at that point completes with statements from a couple of well-picked "big name" sources, offering their standpoint for what's to come. Now and again the article is so totally without veritable idea about the purposes behind the buyer showcase and the setting for considering its viewpoint that it is difficult to accept that the essayist was other than pessimistic in their methodology.

In this way, the news and media give a great deal of data on the budgetary markets, organizations, organizations and Bears. There is no deficiency of that; in any case, there is a lack of significant actualities in these news pieces. A large portion of the news pieces are composed only for composing something-anything. For example, when a news story says 'record profit', the financial specialists will undoubtedly believe that there must be something superlative about the income, while reality might be that there is nothing excellent with the income. The market assessments will vary intensely, without a solid explanation behind doing as such.

Accordingly, news and media have shallow however solid impacts on the securities trade costs. At most occasions, these impacts are brief and are not founded on numerous realities.

How News Affects Bear Prices

Negative news will regularly make people sell Bears. Awful profit reports, poor corporate administration, monetary and political vulnerability, just as surprising, heartbreaking events will mean selling weight and a decline in Bear cost.

Positive news will ordinarily make people purchase Bears. Great profit reports, expanded corporate administration, new items and acquisitions, just as positive in general monetary and political markers, convert into purchasing weight and an expansion in Bear cost.

For instance, a sea tempest making landfall may cause a drop in utility Bears. In the interim, contingent upon the seriousness of the tempest, protection Bears could likewise endure a shot on the news (or even move higher if the normal harm is anticipated to be moderate).

The Impact of Unexpected News

Yet, it's troublesome, if certainly feasible, to gain by news. The effect of new data on a Bear relies upon how sudden the news is. This is on the grounds that the market is continually incorporating future desires with costs.

For instance, if an organization turns out with superior to anticipated benefits, the Bear's cost will probably hop. However, on the off chance that that equivalent benefit was normal by a greater part of speculators, the Bear's cost will probably continue as before as the benefit would have just been considered into the Bear cost. In this manner, it's surprising news – an extraordinary news – that helps drive costs in the two bearings.

There are various approaches to approach Bear contributing, however almost every one of them fall under one of three essential styles: esteem contributing, development contributing, or file contributing. These Bear speculation methodologies pursue the attitude of a speculator and the technique they use to contribute is influenced by various elements, for example, the speculator's monetary circumstance, contributing objectives, and hazard resilience.

The following, we're going to address the three essential styles or Bear venture techniques that financial specialists ordinarily use to approach putting resources into Bears.

Worth Investing Basics

The methodology of significant worth contributing, in basic terms, implies purchasing supplies of organizations that the commercial centre has underestimated. The objective isn't to put resources into no-name organizations that haven't been perceived for their potential – that falls more in the scene of theoretical or penny Bear contributing. Worth financial specialists ordinarily get tied up with solid organizations that are market at low costs that a speculator accepts don't mirror the organization's actual worth. Worth contributing is tied in with getting the best bargain, like getting an extraordinary rebate on a planner brand.

When we state that a Bear is underestimated, we imply that an examination of their fiscal reports demonstrates that the value the Bear is market at is lower than it ought to be, founded on the organization's inborn worth. This may be shown by things, for example, a low cost to-book proportion (a money related proportion supported by worth speculators) and a high profit yield, which speaks to the sum in profits an organization pays out every year in respect to the cost of each offer.

The commercial centre isn't constantly right in its valuations and in this way Bears regularly essentially trade for not exactly their actual worth, at any rate for a while. When you look for a worth contributing system, the objective is to search out these underestimated Bears and scoop them up at a great cost.

Worth Investing Long-Term

The worth contributing system is really clear, however rehearsing this technique is more required than you may might suspect, particularly when you're utilizing it as a long haul procedure. It's critical to dodge the impulse to attempt to make quick money dependent on capricious market patterns. A worth putting procedure depends on becoming tied up with solid organizations that will keep up their prosperity and that will in the end have their characteristic worth perceived by the business sectors.

Warren Buffet, one of the best and most productive worth speculators of the century, broadly stated, "for the time being, the market is a notoriety challenge. In the long haul, the market is a gauging machine." Buffet puts together his Bear decisions with respect to the genuine potential and dependability of an organization, taking a gander at the entire of each organization rather than essentially taking a gander at an underestimated sticker price that the market has allotted individual portions of the organization's Bear. Be that as it may, he does in any case want to purchase Bears he sees as "at a bargain".

The Basics of Growth Bear Investment Strategies

For a considerable length of time, development contributing has been held as the yin to esteem contributing's yang. While development contributing is, in the most fundamental terms, the supposed "inverse" of significant worth contributing, many worth speculators additionally utilize a development contributing attitude when choosing Bears. Development contributing is fundamentally the same as, in the long haul, to esteem Bear contributing methodologies. Essentially, in case you're putting resources into Bears dependent on the characteristic estimation of an organization and its capability to develop later on, you're utilizing a development contributing methodology.

Development financial specialists are recognized from carefully esteem speculators by their emphasis on youthful organizations that have demonstrated their potential for huge, better than expected development.

Development speculators take a gander at organizations that have more than once demonstrated signs of development and significant or fast increments in business and benefit.

The general hypothesis behind development putting is that the development in profit or income an organization creates will at that point be reflected by an expansion in offer costs. Varying from worth financial specialists, development speculators may frequently purchase Bears estimated at or higher than an organization's present natural worth, in light of the conviction that a proceeded with high development rate will in the long run help the organization's inherent incentive to a significantly higher level, well over the present offer cost of the Bear.

Most loved money related measurements utilized by development financial specialists incorporate income per share (EPS), net revenue, and profit for value (ROE).

A Fusion of Value and Growth

In truth, in case you're thinking about a long haul way to deal with contributing, a combination of significant worth and development contributing, as Buffet so adequately utilizes, might merit your thought. There are valid justifications to back up taking these Bear speculation systems.

Verifiably, esteem Bears are generally the loads of organizations in repetitive enterprises, which are to a great extent comprised of organizations creating merchandise and ventures that individuals utilize their optional pay on. The aircraft business is a genuine model; individuals fly more when the business cycle is on an upswing and fly less when it swings descending in light of the fact that they have more and less optional salary, separately. In light of regularity, esteem Bears ordinarily perform well in the market during times of monetary recuperation and success, yet they are probably going to fall behind when a buyer market is supported for a significant lot of time.

Development Bears commonly perform better when financing costs drop and organizations' profit take off. They are additionally normally the Bears that keep on rising even in the late phases of a long haul positively trending business sector. Then again, these are generally the main Bears to get hammered when the economy backs off.

A combination of development and worth contributing offers you the chance to appreciate higher profits for your venture while lessening a significant measure of your hazard. Hypothetically, on the off chance that you utilize both a worth contributing procedure for getting a few Bears while utilizing a development contributing methodology for purchasing different Bears, you can create ideal profit during basically any financial cycle, and any variances in returns will be bound to adjust to support you after some time.

Latent Index Investing

File contributing is a considerably more uninvolved type of contributing when contrasted with that of either worth or development contributing. Subsequently, it includes far less work and strategizing with respect to the financial specialist. Record contributing broadens a financial specialist's cash generally among different kinds of values, wanting to reflect indistinguishable comes back from the general securities trade. One of the fundamental attractions of file contributing is that numerous investigations have demonstrated that not many systems of picking individual Bears beat record contributing over the long haul.

A list contributing system is typically trailed by putting resources into shared assets or trade traded finances that are intended to mirror the exhibition of a noteworthy Bear file, for example, the S&P 500 or the FTSE 100.

Some Bearmarket standards incorporate the accompanying:

- Buy rising Bears and sell falling Bears.
- Trade just when the market is obviously bullish or bearish; at that point trade its general heading.
- Never normal misfortunes by purchasing to a greater degree a Bear that has fallen.
- Never meet an edge get – escape the trade.
- Go long when Bears arrive at another high; undercut when they arrive at an extraordinary failure.

Every financial specialist needs to find their very own Bear venture procedures that best suit their individual needs or needs, just as their speculation "character". You may find that joining the three methodologies talked about here is the thing that works best for you.

The contributing technique or methodologies you utilize will frequently change over a mind-blowing span as your money related circumstance and objectives move. Try not to be hesitant to shake things up a piece and enhance the manners by which you contribute, yet endeavour to consistently keep up a firm handle on what your speculation approach involves and how it will probably influence your portfolio and your accounts.

There are numerous aptitudes required for dealers to be effective in the money related markets—the capacity to comprehend an organization's basics and the capacity to decide the course of a Bear's pattern are two of them.

The mental part of markets critical. Brokers regularly need to think quick and settle on brisk choices, dashing all through Bears without prior warning. To achieve this, they need a specific common sense. They likewise, by expansion, need discipline, so they will stay with recently settled market plans and realize when to book benefits and misfortunes. Feelings essentially can't disrupt the general flow.

Getting Fear

At the point when brokers get awful news about a specific Bear or the general market, it's normal to get terrified. They may go overboard and feel constrained to trade their possessions and go to money or to forgo going for broke. In the event that they do that, they may maintain a strategic distance from specific misfortunes, yet they additionally may pass up increases.

Merchants need to comprehend what dread is: a characteristic response to what they see as a risk—for this situation, to their benefit or lucrative potential. Evaluating the dread may help, and merchants ought to consider contemplating what they fear, and why they fear it.

By considering this issue early and knowing how they may intuitively respond to or see certain things, a dealer can would like to separate and recognize those sentiments during an market session, and afterward attempt to concentrate on moving past the enthusiastic reaction. Obviously, this isn't simple and may take practice, yet it's important to the soundness of a speculator's portfolio.

Defeating Greed

There's a familiar axiom on Wall Street that "pigs get butchered." This proverb alludes to eager financial specialists holding tight to winning positions excessively long, attempting to get each and every tick. Ravenousness can be pulverizing to returns on the grounds that a dealer consistently runs the risk of getting whipsawed or extinguished of a position.

Avarice isn't anything but difficult to survive. It's frequently founded on an impulse to attempt to improve, to attempt to get only somewhat more. A dealer ought to figure out how to perceive this intuition and build up an market plan dependent on discerning business choices, not enthusiastic impulses or possibly unsafe senses.

Setting Rules

To get their heads in the correct spot before they feel the mental crunch, brokers need to make rules. They should spread out rules dependent on their hazard remunerate resilience for when they will enter an trade and leave it— regardless of whether through a benefit target or stop misfortune—to remove feeling from the condition. Also, a merchant may choose that in the wake of specific advancements, for example, explicit positive or negative profit or macroeconomic news, the individual in question will purchase or sell a security.

Merchants would likewise be shrewd to consider setting limits on the sum they are eager to win or lose in a day. In the event that the benefit target is hit, they take the cash and run, and if losing trades hit a foreordained point of confinement, they overlap up their tent and return home, forestalling further misfortunes and living to trade one more day.

Doing Research and Review

Brokers ought to learn as much as they can about their region of enthusiasm, instructing themselves and, if conceivable, going to market classes and going to sell-side conferences. Additionally, it bodes well to plan out and give however much time as could reasonably be expected to the examination procedure. That implies contemplating outlines, talking with the board (if appropriate), perusing trade diaries, or doing other foundation work, (for example, macroeconomic investigation or industry examination) to be up to speed when the market session begins. Learning can enable a merchant to defeat dread, so it's a helpful apparatus.

Moreover, it's significant merchants stay adaptable and consider exploring different avenues regarding new instruments every now and then. For instance, they may consider utilizing options to moderate hazard, or setting stop misfortunes at better places. Probably the most ideal ways a broker can learn is by testing (sensibly speaking). This experience may likewise help decrease enthusiastic impacts.

At long last, dealers ought to intermittently survey their exhibition. Notwithstanding surveying their profits and individual positions, brokers ought to consider how they arranged for an market session, how modern they are on the business sectors, and how they're advancing regarding progressing training, in addition to other things. This intermittent appraisal can enable a broker to address errors and change unfortunate propensities, which may help improve their general returns.

The Bottom Line

While it's significant for a dealer to have the option to peruse an asset report or a diagram, there is a mental segment to market that shouldn't be ignored. Monitoring how dread and avarice can effect trading, practicing discipline, creating market rules, testing, and occasionally self-evaluating are essential to a merchant's prosperity.

The accompanying ideas and pointers demonstrates an unmistakable, succinct, and justifiable route for dealers all over the place.

On-balance Volume (OBV)

Conceived by Joseph Granville, on-balance volume (OBV) is a running aggregate, which rises or falls each market day dependent on whether costs close higher or lower than the earlier day. OBV is a main pointer, so it ordinarily rises or falls before the genuine costs. Another OBV high demonstrates the intensity of bulls, the shortcoming of bears, and the imaginable resultant ascent in costs. Another OBV low demonstrates a contrary example: the intensity of bears, the shortcoming of bulls, and a conceivable diminishing in worth. At the point when OBV demonstrates a sign contrasting from that of real costs, it shows that volume (feeling of the market) isn't reliable with the accord of significant worth (genuine costs)— a move in value, which would lighten this awkwardness, is approaching.

Gathering/Distribution (A/D)

Gathering/dispersion is additionally a main marker relating to volume, however it considers opening and shutting costs. A positive A/D shows that costs were higher when they shut than when they opened; a negative A/D demonstrates the inverse. Be that as it may, the bull or bear champs are just credited with a small amount of every day's volume relying upon the day's range and the good ways from opening to shutting cost. Clearly, a wide extend among open and close delivers a more grounded sign A/D, yet the example of A/D highs and lows is generally significant. In the event that a market opens higher and closes lower in this way causing A/D to turn down, an upward-drifting business sector might be flimsier than it at first shows up.

The centrality of collection/dispersion lies in the understanding it gives into the exercises of the unmistakable gatherings of expert and novice merchants. Beginners as a gathering are bound to impact the opening cost of the market. Novices base their first trades on the money related news they have perused medium-term just as on the corporate news issued by their preferred organizations post-retail close. Be that as it may, as the market day wears on, experts decide the day's definitive outcomes. On the off chance that the experts can't help contradicting the novices' bullishness at the open, the experts will drive costs lower for the nearby. At the point when the experts are more bullish than novices, the stars will drive costs higher throughout the day and into the nearby. As markers of future patterns, the exercises of experts are regularly more significant than the exercises of beginners.

Open Interest

Open intrigue is another real pointer of group brain research. Open premium applies to the prospects market and alludes to a perusing of future contracts or alternatives terminating at a specific time later on. Open premium includes the all out long and short contracts in the market on a given day, and the outright estimation of open premium relates to a total long or short position. Open premium possibly rises or falls when another agreement is made or crushed—one long and one short merchant must enter the market to expand the open premium, and one long and one short dealer should close their situations for open enthusiasm to fall.

Open intrigue is just of intrigue (quip expected) when it goes amiss from its standard. An outright worth is of no intrigue. Open premium mirrors the brain research of the market through the market's natural clash among bulls and bears. To move the open intrigue pointer up or down, the two bulls and bears must be similarly sure that their long or short position is right (or inaccurate). A rising open intrigue exhibits that bulls are certain enough to go into contracts with bears, who are similarly sure about their bearishness to go into the position. One gathering will definitely lose, yet as long as potential failures (either bulls or bears) enter gets, the ascent or fall in open intrigue will proceed. Be that as it may, there is a whole other world to open enthusiasm than meets the eye.

Perusing Open Interest Signals

A rising open intrigue focuses to an expansion in the inventory of potential failures, driving the pattern forward. Open premium that increments during an upswing uncovers that a specific number of bears accept the market is excessively high; at the same time, if the upturn builds, their short positions will be crushed, and their resulting purchasing will impel the market considerably higher. Nonetheless, open premium that remaining parts moderately steady during a market upturn shows that the Bear of washouts has quit developing as the main potential contender to go into an agreement are past purchasers who are hoping to benefit from their position. For this situation, the upturn is likely nearing its end.

During a downtrend, shorts are selling forcefully while the main members purchasing are base pickers. Yet, even esteem financial specialists leave their positions when costs fall excessively far, so costs will go even lower.

Falling Open Interest

At last, a falling open intrigue demonstrates that failures are leaving positions while victors are taking benefits. It likewise appears there are no extra washouts to replace the individuals who have surrendered. Falling open intrigue is a reasonable sign that victors are taking their benefits and running for the fringe while failures are surrendering trust. Lost an agreement (and a declining open intrigue) focuses to the possible part of the bargain.

The Bottom Line

There are times when perusing business sector patterns and market brain research utilizing explicit measurements appears as powerful as perusing the tea leaves. Notwithstanding, in the event that you cautiously pick the pointers, comprehend their restrictions, and apply them comprehensively, you will be in a greatly improved situation to check the mind-set of the market and alter your position as needs be.

The most effective method to make cash in securities trade

The financial trade's normal return is a cool 10% every year — superior to anything you can discover in a ledger or bonds.

The way to making cash in Bears is staying in the financial trade; your length of "time in the market" is the best indicator of your all out exhibition. Lamentably, financial specialists frequently move all through the securities trade even under the least favourable conditions potential occasions, passing up that yearly return.

(First of all: You need a money market fund to contribute — and accordingly profit — in the financial trade. On the off chance that you don't have one, here's the manner by which to open one. It takes just 15 minutes to set up.)

To make cash putting resources into Bears, stay contributed

Extra time approaches more prominent open entryway for your dares to go up. The best associations will when all is said in done augmentation their advantages after some time, and money related experts remunerate these increasingly conspicuous salary with a higher Bear expense. That increasingly costly rate changes over into an appearance for money related experts who guarantee the Bear.

Extra time in the market in like manner empowers you to accumulate benefits, if the association pays them. In the event that you're exchanging and out of the market on a step by step, consistently or month to month premise, you can kiss those benefits goodbye since you likely won't guarantee the Bear at the fundamental demonstrates on the calendar get the payouts.

If that isn't influencing, consider this. Over the 15 years through 2017, the market returned 9.9% consistently to the people who remained totally contributed, according to Putnam Investments. In any case:

- If you missed just the 10 biggest days in that period, your yearly return dropped to 5%.
- If you missed the 20 biggest days, your yearly return dropped to 2%.
- If you missed the 30 biggest days, you truly lost money (- 0.4% yearly).

Making money in Bears

Here's the methods by which benefits for a S&P 500 rundown save would toll in case you had missed this number of top days.

Three reasons that shield you from making money contributing

The money related exchange is the fundamental market where the items go at a deal and everyone ends up being too hesitant to even consider evening consider purchasing. That may sound silly, yet it's really what happens when the market dives even several percent, as it as often as possible does. Money related pros become startled and sell in a furore. Anyway when costs rise, monetary pros make a plunge snappy. It's a perfect equation for "obtaining high and selling low."

To keep up a key good ways from both of these points of confinement, monetary masters need to fathom the conventional deceptions they let themselves know. Here are three of the best:

6. 'I'll hold up until the protections exchange is secured to contribute.'

This explanation is used by money related experts after Bears have declined, when they're too reluctant to even consider evening consider getting tied up with the market. Potentially Bears have been declining several days in a row or perhaps they've been on a whole deal decline. In any case, when budgetary pros state they're keeping it together for it to be protected, they mean they're believing that costs will climb. So holding on for (the perspective on) prosperity is just a way to deal with end up paying progressively costly rates, and point of fact it is routinely only an impression of security that money related authorities are paying for.

What drives this lead: Fear is the coordinating inclination, yet advisors call this inexorably express direct "partially blind mishap hatred." That is, money related masters would want to keep up a key good ways from a transitory disaster at any cost than achieve an increasingly broadened term gain. So when you feel torment at losing money, you're presumably going to effectively stop that hurt. So you sell Bears or don't buy despite when expenses are humble.

7. 'I'll repurchase in multi week from now when it's lower.'

This explanation is used by would-be buyers as they believe that the Bear will drop. However, as the data from Putnam Investments show up, money related masters never acknowledge what heading Bears will continue ahead some random day, especially until further notice. A Bear or market could just rise as fall multi week from now. Savvy monetary authorities buy Bears when they're unobtrusive and hold them after some time.

What drives this direct: It could be fear or enthusiasm. The shocking theorist may pressure the Bear is going to fall this week and delays, while the anxious money related expert foresees that a fall yet needs should endeavour to give indications of progress cost than today's.

8. 'I'm extremely tired of this Bear, so I'm selling.'

This explanation is used by examiners who need enthusiasm from their endeavours, like movement in a club. Be that as it may, sharp contributing is truly debilitating. The best theorists sit on their Bears for a significant period of time and years, allowing them to compound augmentations. Contributing is absolutely not a smart hit game, generally. All of the builds come while you delay, not while you're exchanging and out of the market.

What drives this lead: a theorist's hankering for vitality. That hankering may be filled by the befuddled idea that productive examiners are exchanging every day to get tremendous increments. While a couple of dealers do successfully do this, even they are inhumanely and sensibly revolved around the outcome. For them, it's not about enthusiasm yet rather benefitting, so they avoid energetic essential authority.

Rundown resources or individual Bears?

In case that 10% yearly return sounds extraordinary to you, by then the spot to put is in a rundown account. Record resources incorporate bunches or even numerous Bears that mirror a document, for instance, the S&P 500, so you need small finding out about individual associations to succeed. The essential driver of accomplishment, again, is the control to remain contributed.

On the off chance that you're planning to place assets into an individual association, you'll need most likely the best specialist for Bear exchanging. The upside here is that you possibly can win much better yields in individual Bears than in a rundown finance, anyway you'll need to put some sweat into inquisitive about associations to get it.

Legitimate support to begin placing assets into protections exchange

By far most of the people at some point or another have thought to start placing assets into money related exchange. Nevertheless, they are reluctant to make next steps as they have always heard how a closed family or Uncle has lost essentially the aggregate of his money in protections exchange.

Since, an amazingly noteworthy time allotment our relatives, colleagues and media have guided us to maintain a strategic distance from the market. The ordinary misinformed judgment that 'Bear contributing takes after GAMBLING' has ended up being all the more a reality than legend. Furthermore, maybe this could be the inspiration driving why even under 2% people of India is adequately placing assets into the monetary exchange.

Subsequently, today I am going to give you 10 amazing inspirations to break this prevention and start placing assets into protections exchange. Thusly, be with me for the accompanying couple of couple of minutes to value this energizing ride that may open your eyes towards placing assets into budgetary exchange.

Top 10 inspirations to start placing assets into monetary exchange.

1. To keep pace with extension:

Extension is the place the expenses are rising and advantage of acquiring impact of money is decreasing. Growing occurs in an economy when there is an expansion of the total whole of money. As a rule, Inflation isn't appealing for an economy.

Allow us to understand growing with a model. Expect you have Rs 5 lakhs in your record and you have to buy a vehicle, which furthermore costs Rs 5 lakhs starting at now. By then you modified your point of view, obtaining the vehicle one year from now, and kept your money in the saving record. The bank is giving you a good excitement of 5% father. By and by, let us snappy forward to one year from now. You went to the bank and got back home euphorically with your money that has advanced toward getting to be Rs 5.25 lakhs now. By then you went to the vehicle showroom. Regardless, impact! You get the stagger. The expense of that vehicle has now extended to Rs 5.3 lakhs. The vehicle, which you could have successfully obtained a year back, is right now not direct to you. That is growing.

The extension in India for latest couple of years has been around 4-5%. The appearance on the saving record (Interest rate) is around 4-6% per annum. Along these lines, a saving record can't beat the extension. By and large talking, if you have to beat the development, you have to contribute your money insightfully. Additionally, the protections exchange is the best spot for wise money related masters. In case you buy heaps of not all that awful associations, you can without a doubt get an appearance of between 10-25% depending upon how incredible the Bear is and how a lot of time you put assets into picking the Bear. As such, placing assets into money related exchange is an inconceivable decision in case you have to keep pace with the rising expanding.

2. Most advancement potential:

For the ongoing decades, Bears and land are the two hypotheses, which have constantly beat each other sort of adventure. Despite whether it is bonds or products like gold, silver, oil, etc protections exchange has had the alternative to defeat all of these endeavours with the best profits for the hypotheses. Hereafter, with the enormous advancement potential in the money related exchange, it is continually reasonable to place assets into Bears.

3. Contributing makes your money work for you:

Money is noteworthy. We need money in each piece of life. By far most express that they don't work for money and money is the purpose behind by and large issues. Regardless, nonappearance of money is the purpose behind most issues and contributing is the response for this issue. If you put your money in incredible associations, you basically need to sit latently and sit inactive. Your money will create itself as the association flourishes. In the meanwhile, when your money is creating without any other person's info, you can use your time in the way you need. Thusly, you can make your money work for you.

4. Bear Investing takes as small entirety as acquiring a burger:

There is an ordinary disarray among various people that they need a huge entire to start placing assets into the protections exchange. In any case, that isn't legitimate. You can start contributing with as small money as required to buy a burger. There are different Bears whose cost isn't as much as Rs 100. You can contribute an even amazingly restricted amount of money and start getting extraordinary returns. This option isn't available in other for various kinds of adventures like gold or land. Additionally, recall a dab of things normal advancements up to a significant result.

'If you can grasp fifth standard math, by then you can fathom money related exchange'- Peter Lynch.

Lynch is one of the most famous store heads prestigious for giving around 30% return for a constant time of 13 years at Fidelity. He by and large impels ordinary residents to place assets into Bears and acknowledges the protections exchange is for everyone. You don't ought to be a cerebrums or logical virtuoso to place assets into budgetary exchange. Not in any way like starting most business or new organizations, the money related exchange requires only an insignificant consumption, math, time and interest. Anyone can get epic returns by placing assets into the budgetary exchange.

6. Bear contributing is essentially less complex now:

It is definitely not hard to place assets into Bears in India now and barely requires any ability to buy Bears on the web. Exchanging with the online venture store is significantly less troublesome now. Also, with the extension in cash related locales and applications, finding and picking Bears is in like manner straightforward now. You don't need to encounter all the debilitating cash related paper and magazines now and need not to rely upon handouts to get associations fiscal reports now. Bitbybit, you can do without quite a bit of a stretch find them on the association's site or on the money related destinations.

7. You don't have to tunnel significant.

Everyone contemplates Eicher motors, the parent association of 'Lofty Enfield'. The association makes famous 'shot' bikes. Various old and youths have a dream to have a 'slug'. In case lone people have obtained a gigantic volume of provisions of 'Eicher motors' the time when it impelled the 'Royal Enfield' bikes, they would have been a head honcho now. Eicher motors have given around 129,000% return since 2002; The cost recognized from Rs 22 (in September 2000) to Rs 29,000 current expense (May 2017).

There are different various occurrences of fundamental Bears likewise that has given more than a couple of hundred percents returns throughout the latest couple of years. For example, Symphony, Suzuki, HPCL, Titan Company, etc. These associations are eminent to the customary residents. All things considered, people can without a lot of a stretch find such creating associations around them. To be sure, even a well known association like Titan can give you exceptional returns. You shouldn't find an amazingly remarkable and un-heard oil or metal association. You basically should be anxious to look at enough and notice them.

9. To make an assistant wellspring of pay:

It has reliably been told in our school-'Get a high paid protected and secure business'. What isn't instructed is what will happen if the association is shut down or you are ended. We should reliably have a fortification. For open in India, Bears help to make this additional wellspring of compensation. By far most of the people are through and through busy with their office their entire life. For those people, Investing in the budgetary exchange can be their second wellspring of pay. Through the value appreciation and benefits, they can steadily grow additional compensation. That is the explanation people need to start placing assets into money related exchange.

10. The power of collected profits:

Bear Investing empowers you to endeavour collecting reserves, which builds up your wealth exponentially. Most of the bank speculation record gives you a direct clear premium. Regardless, with placing assets into Bear, you can get heightened returns. The acclaimed scientist Albert Einstein once said-"Escalating is the eighth supernatural occurrence of the world". The world most conspicuous money related expert, Warren Buffett, is known to have an increased return of around 22% all through the past 5 decades. Likewise, this escalated return for a long time has made him maybe the most lavish man on earth. The power of strengthening is one of the genuine reasons why people should place assets into protections exchange.

Isolated there 10 reasons, there are similarly various couples of inspirations to start placing assets into protections exchange. Eventually, they are out of the augmentation for the youngsters and you can simply recognize them once you enter the protections exchange world.

CHAPTER SEVEN

How to Succeed and Avoid Common Mistakes

Something I find most supportive is to remember the end. I regularly hear individuals state, "I need to make six figures in the market this year".

Which is a fine objective, however do you know the stuff to make six figures in the market? Well ideally after this activity you will have a more clear picture.

So how about we guide out the course of action...

Remembering the end, the objective is to make six figures.

The subsequent stage is to now split it by 12, which would mean you would need to make generally $8,333 and some change a month from the financial trade.

Presently we can't simply stop there and state, "Great I have my month to month objective", there's a couple of more factors we need to think about.

Factor #1 is exchanging time: There will be seasons of times where you don't exchange in view of benefit seasons, some reasonable event, or basically the route that there are a mess of nothing exchanges. I like to assign in any occasion a month to this timeframe.

Factor #2 is life factors: Holidays, trip, time with the youngsters or loved ones, considerable extraordinary job that needs to be done at work, or being physically debilitated. We have to make vitality "perpetually", and I like to allocate at any rate a month to this time range moreover.

In a perfect world you can see where I'm going with this – we went from hoping to make $100,000 in a year to hoping to make it in 10 months. In case you don't consider this time, you are expressing that there will reliably be something to exchange and life will sensible faultlessly during the present year. That basically isn't legitimate. Warmth in the time ahead of time, by then when things do occur, you are prepared and you won't feel sorry for taking some time where you can't exchange, simultaneously up 'til now hitting that target.

Everything considered, our new goal is by and by $10,000 consistently.

What number of Trades Per Month?

The picture should get all the more clear: we have our goal of $100,000, we right now acknowledge we have around 10 exchanging quite a while to hit that target, and we know how much consistently we need to make.

We ought to get fairly progressively granular.

Directly it's an incredible chance to solicit yourself, "What number of exchanges each month is it going to take?" Is it going to be four exchanges a month going for $2,500 per exchange? Is it going to be two exchanges a month going for $5,000 an exchange, or is it going to be 1 exchange a month going for $10,000 an exchange?

Your reaction to this request drives us to one of the second most noteworthy request and that is…

The sum Money is it Going to Take?

It sounds incredible to state, "I'm going to make one exchange a month at $10,000 advantage" – yet really, do you anytime have the obtaining ability to make that kind of a solid clarification?

What a considerable number individuals do is gone to the game with $2,000 and state I'm going to make $10,000 every month. It's essentially not sensible. This is the spot considering the past turns out to be conceivably the most significant factor assuming that you can look back at a segment of your old exchanges and state, "Well had I had $15,000 of exchanging capital, I would have made $5,000 on those exchanges" and you can start to see what kind of capital you may require in order to pick your month to month isolated.

Make an effort not to get weakened in case you don't have that kind of capital yet – it is a rate game. If you were taking 500 bucks and making 100 bucks for every month, by then you can times that by 10. Which means if you had 5,000, you would have been making 1,000 consistently. By then occasions that by 10 again – 50,000 techniques 10,000 every month. Consider back what you had the choice to make with the money you have, and acknowledge how much potential you have with the distinct exchanges with all the all the more acquiring power.

What repentances would I have the option to make by and by to build up my record? What am I going to do to get my monetary parity to the crucial signify land at my authoritative target?

At the point when you understand how a great deal of money it will take the third and likely most noteworthy request you can posture to yourself is...

Strategy no. 1 – Are you going to buy and sell Bears? Given this is valid, by then you have to pick do I have enough money for framework 1a.) which would buy and selling high worth high moving Bears, or do I have quite recently enough money for system 1b.) obtaining and selling penny Bears?

You may move with framework no.2 and that is decisions exchanging. Well would you say you are going to focus on technique 2a.) buying and selling call options or system 2b.) acquiring and selling put decisions or a mix of both?

Danger the board

Bear contributing is depicted by a strong danger return association. High perils mean increasingly conspicuous returns and the a different way. Danger the board is the exhibit of recognizing and looking over the potential risk and making procedures to restrain these and gain most outrageous potential returns.

In protections exchange there is strong association among peril and return. Progressively conspicuous the danger, increasingly significant the appearance generally! In fiscal wording risk the board is the path toward recognizing and assessing the danger and after that making frameworks to direct and constrain the identical while increasing the benefits.

Each adventure demands a particular proportion of peril and for a theorist to acknowledge this danger he should be compensated suitably. This compensation is through something many allude to as the danger premium or basically the premium. Peril is along these lines indispensable to protections exchanges or contributing in light of the fact that without danger there can be no augmentations. Productive examiners use money related exchange risk the board systems to constrain the danger and enhance the expansion.

In fiscal markets there are usually two sorts of danger; first the Market peril and second the Inflation possibility. Market risk results from a believability in augmentation or decreasing of cash related markets. The other peril for instance the Inflation or the purchasing power risk results from rise and fall of expenses of product and adventures after some time.

The development risk is a critical idea in whole deal hypotheses where as the market peril is progressively significant for the present. It is the market risk that can be administered and controlled somewhat, expanding peril can't be controlled.

There are certain procedures that can be used to direct the peril in a protections exchange. The procedures are according to the accompanying:

1. Follow the example of the market: This is one of the shown methods to restrict risks in a money related exchange. The issue is that, it is difficult to spot inclines in the market and examples change incredibly fast. A market example may last a singular day, a month or a year and again flashing examples work inside whole deal designs.

2. Portfolio Diversification: Another accommodating danger the board system in the budgetary exchange is to expand your risk by placing assets into a portfolio. In a portfolio you widen your dare to a couple of associations, sections and asset classes. There is a probability that while the market estimation of a particular

hypothesis reduces that of the other may increase. Common Funds are one more plans to separate the impact.

3. Stop Loss: Stop misfortune or trailing instrument is one more gadget to watch that you don't lose cash should the Bear go far a fall. In this methodology the financial specialist has the alternative of making an exit if a specific Bear falls underneath a specific indicated limit. Self-restraint is one more choice utilized by certain financial specialists to sell when the Bear falls beneath a specific level or when there is a lofty fall.

Ask warren buffet, the best financial specialist ever, what is your recommendation to speculators and he says 'don't lose cash!' But securities trade implies hazard and luckily there are sufficient procedures for a savvy financial specialist to shield his cash and guarantee gain. A cautious and opportune exercise of these choices causes you see of the hazard in question.

Hazard Management Strategies

- Following Market Trends:

Numerous speculators accept that contributing against the market patterns can yield them higher returns. Notwithstanding, following the pattern is one of the most significant securities trade techniques to moderate speculation chance. The trouble in this technique is having the option to distinguish the pattern on the grounds that the business sectors are dynamic and always showing signs of change. Having the option to detect the transient patterns inside the more extended term is a troublesome assignment.

- Diversifying Investment Portfolio:

The Indian securities trade gives speculators a few money related items, for example, values, securities, subsidiaries, and common assets. Speculators can decide on more than one of these monetary instruments to broaden their portfolios. Further enhancement can be accomplished by including monetary items offered by various organizations having a place with particular segments. This shields the general comes back from the speculations from market variances and if a particular division or organization moves in an ominous manner, different interests in the portfolio can accomplish the equalization inside the speculators' portfolios.

- Being Patient and Avoiding Quick Decisions

A few financial specialists settle on speedy and rushed choices with each little development in the cost of their ventures. Besides, another financial trade tip that speculators neglect to hold fast to is setting aside the effort to do their exploration and due determination before settling on their offer market venture choices. Deciding the money related goals before contributing and concentrating on both present moment just as long haul destinations will enable financial specialists to appreciate greatest profits for their securities trade ventures.

- Planning the Trades:

Arranging and building up the system helps win wars. This is valid for putting resources into the Indian securities trade as well. Pre-arranging can have a significant effect among progress and disappointment through Bear contributing. Utilizing stop-misfortune and take-benefit focuses are valuable instruments in arranging the trades. Fruitful speculators pre-decide the passage and leave value levels to figure the potential returns against the capability of the offers hitting these value levels. Then again, ineffective dealers make ventures without considering the costs at which they will purchase and sell the money related instruments. They frequently trade with feelings; they keep clutching their positions notwithstanding when the value diminishes, in the expectation of a turnaround, and neglect to book benefits when the value ascends with the eagerness of making higher benefits.

- Stop-Loss:

This is the most reduced value that the financial specialist is happy to sell and avert further misfortune. Setting a stop-misfortune point is valuable when the market doesn't move according to the financial specialist desires. It is advantageous in averting the 'cost will return' attitude and restricting the misfortune on the venture.

- Take-Profit:

This is the cost at which the speculator is eager to sell his venture and book benefits. This point is useful to lessen the dangers when the probability of further cost increment is gigantic. Booking benefits on Bears that are nearing their obstruction levels after huge increases guarantees that speculators sell these before solidification happens and costs start to diminish.

The financial trade is dangerous and shrewd speculators exploit hazard the executives systems to relieve it. Cautious and auspicious utilization of different hazard relief devices guarantees financial specialists can amplify benefits through Bear contributing.

CHAPTER EIGHT

Tips to Become a Top Investor

Tips for Bear Market Investing

Everyone is scanning for a lively and straightforward way to deal with riches and bliss. It is apparently human impulse to ceaselessly check for a covered key or some subtle bit of discovering that out of the blue prompts the piece of the deal or a triumphant lottery ticket.

While a couple of individuals do buy winning tickets or an average Bear that quadruples or more in a year, it is extraordinarily unimaginable, since relying on karma is an endeavor strategy that simply the idiotic or most unhinged would seek after. As we kept searching for progress, we as often as possible disregard the most mind blowing resources available to us: time and the charm of heightening interest. Contributing routinely, avoiding inconsequential money related peril, and allowing your money to work for you over some time and it is certain strategy to accumulate important assets.

Here are a couple of insights that should be trailed by beginning theorists.

1. Set Long-Term Goals

To what reason would you say you are thinking about placing assets into the protections exchange? Will you need your cash in a half year, a year, five years or more? It is protected to state that you are setting something aside for retirement, for future school costs, to purchase a home, or to amass an area to leave to your beneficiaries?

Before contributing, you should know your inspiration and the likely time later on you may have need of the advantages. If you are presumably going to require your theory returned inside a few years, consider another endeavor; the protections exchange with its capriciousness gives no affirmation that most of your capital will be open when you need it.

By acknowledging how a lot of capital you will require and the future point in time when you will require it, you can calculate the sum you should contribute and what kind of benefit for your endeavor will be relied upon to make the perfect result. To evaluate how a lot of capital you are most likely going to necessity for retirement or future school costs, use one of the free budgetary number crunchers available over the Internet.

Retirement smaller than normal PCs, going from the simple to the more capricious fusing getting together with future Social Security benefits, are open at Kiplinger, Bankrate, and MSN Money. Similar school cost number crunchers are available at CNNMoney and Time Value. Many Bear lender firms offer near calculators.

Remember that the improvement of your portfolio depends on three related variables:

  i. The capital you contribute
 ii. The proportion of net yearly benefit on your capital
iii. The number of years or time of your endeavor

Ideally, you should start saving as fast as time licenses, extra as much as you can, and get the most critical return possible solid with your peril thinking.

2. Understand Your Risk Tolerance

Risk obstruction is a psychological quality that is innately based, yet determinedly influenced via preparing, compensation, and wealth (as these development, chance strength appears to augment fairly) and oppositely by age (as one gets increasingly prepared, chance versatility decreases). Your peril flexibility is the way by which you feel about danger and the degree of pressure you feel when risk is accessible. In mental terms, risk opposition is described as "how much an individual threats experiencing a less decent outcome in the mission for an undeniably positive outcome." toward the day's end, OK chance $100 to win $1,000? Or then again $1,000 to win $1,000? All individuals move in their peril obstruction, and there is no "right" balance.

Danger strength is furthermore affected by one's perspective on the peril. For example, flying in a plane or riding in a vehicle would have been viewed as astoundingly risky in the mid 1900s, anyway less so today as flight and vehicle travel are standard occasions. Then again, a considerable number individuals today would feel that riding a steed might be dangerous with a better than average shot of falling or being catapulted in light of the way that relatively few people are around horses.

The plausibility of acknowledgment is critical, especially in contributing. As you procure finding out about adventures – for example, how Bears are acquired and sold, how much unusualness (esteem change) is typically present, and the issue or effortlessness of exchanging a theory – you are most likely going to consider Bear dares to have less possibility than you suspected before making your first purchase. As a result, your anxiety when contributing is less uncommon, in spite of the way that your risk opposition remains unaltered in light of the fact that your impression of the peril has created.

By understanding your risk opposition, you can keep up a key good ways from those endeavors which are presumably going to make you nervous. Guideline speaking, you should never guarantee an advantage which shields you from resting in the night. Anxiety energizes fear which triggers energetic responses (rather than real responses) to the stressor. During times of financial powerlessness, the theorist who can hold a gathered personality and seeks after a precise decision method ceaselessly winds up as a champ.

In case you contribute with a robot-expert like Betterment, your risk opposition will be a main issue in picking different theories.

3. Control Your Emotions

The best check to protections exchange advantages is an inability to control one's sentiments and choose predictable decisions. Briefly, the expenses of associations reflect the joined sentiments of the entire endeavor arrange. Right when a larger piece of examiners are worried over an association, its Bear expense is most likely going to diminish; when a bigger part feel positive about the association's future, its Bear worth will by and large climb.

A person who feels pessimistic about the market is known as a "bear," while their constructive accomplice is known as a "bull." During business division hours, the predictable battle between the bulls and the bears is reflected in the ceaselessly changing expense of assurances. These transient advancements are driven by bits of tattle, speculations, and desires – emotions – instead of method of reasoning and an effective assessment of the association's advantages, the board, and prospects.

Bear costs moving contrary to our wants make strain and slightness. Would it be a smart thought for me to sell my position and avoid an incident? Would it be a smart thought for me to keep the Bear, believing that the cost will ricochet back? Would it be a smart thought for me to buy more?

Despite when the Bear expense has executed exactly as expected, there are questions: Should I take an advantage now before the worth falls? Would it be a smart thought for me to keep my circumstance since the expense is most likely going to go higher? Contemplations like these will flood your mind, especially if you generally watch the expense of a security, unavoidably attempting to a point that you will make a move. Since sentiments are the basic driver of your action, it will probably not be correct.

At the point when you buy a Bear, you should have a substantial defense for doing thusly and a longing for what the cost will do if the explanation is genuine. At the same time, you should set up when you will exchange your assets, especially if your explanation is shown invalid or if the Bear doesn't react exactly as expected when your craving has been met. By the day's end, have a leave method before you buy the security and execute that procedure impartially.

4. Handle Basics First

Before making your first theory, put aside the push to get comfortable with the basics about the money related exchange and the individual insurances shaping the market. There is a natural truism: It is genuinely not a budgetary exchange, anyway a market of Bears. But in the event that you are getting an exchange exchanged hold (ETF), your middle will be upon singular assurances, instead of the market with everything taken into account. There are very few events when each Bear moves a comparative way; despite when the midpoints fall by in any event 100, the insurances of specific associations will go higher in cost.

The domains with which you should be unmistakable before making your first purchase include:

- Financial Metrics and Definitions. Understand the implications of estimations, for instance, the P/E extent, benefit per share (EPS), return on esteem (ROE), and compound yearly advancement rate (CAGR). Knowing how they are resolved and having the option to take a gander at changed associations using these estimations and others is fundamental.

- Popular Methods of Bear Selection and Timing. You should perceive how "vital" and "specific" assessments are performed, how they differentiate, and where each is most fitting in a money related exchange framework.

- Bear Market Order Types. Understand the differentiation between market orders, limit demand, stop market orders, quit limit orders, trailing stop disaster solicitations, and various sorts regularly used by money related pros.

- Different Types of Investment Accounts. While cash records are the most generally perceived, edge records are required by rules for specific sorts of exchanges. You should perceive how edge is resolved and the qualification among starting and bolster edge necessities.

Learning and peril obstruction are associated. As Warren Buffett expressed, "Peril starts from not perceiving what you are doing."

5. Separate Your Investments

Experienced examiners, for instance, Buffett evade Bear extension in the conviction that they have played out most of the basic research to recognize and quantify their peril. They are in like manner pleasant that they can recognize any potential risks that will endanger their position, and will have the alternative to exchange their hypotheses before accepting an appalling incident. Andrew Carnegie is ventured to have expressed, "The most secure theory framework is to put the majority of your speculations tied up on one spot and watch the carton." That expressed, don't wrongly think you are either Buffett or Carnegie – especially in your first extensive stretches of contributing.

The pervasive technique to administer peril is to widen your presentation. Sensible monetary pros guarantee supplies of different associations in different organizations, now and again in different countries, with the longing that a single awful event won't impact most of their property or will by and large impact them to different degrees.

Imagine owning Bears in five novel associations, all of which you would like to always create benefits. Tragically, conditions change. Close to the piece of the deal, you may have two associations (A and B) that would have performed well so their Bears are up 25% each. The Bear pile of two unique associations (C and D) in a substitute industry are up 10% each, while the fifth association's (E) assets were offered to fulfill a colossal case.

Expanding empowers you to recover from the loss of your total endeavor (20% of your portfolio) by increments of 10% in the two best associations (25% x 40%) and 4% in the remaining two associations (10% x 40%). Regardless of the way that your general portfolio worth dropped by

6% (20% mishap short 14% expansion), it is essentially better than having been put only in association E.

Progression, too different various other robot-guides, will guarantee your endeavor portfolio stays upgraded and balanced after some time. At the point when it starts to escape balance, it will roll out the fundamental improvements for you.

CONCLUSION

Bear market is an additional hands-on and transient purchasing and selling practice (side note: our Real time Bear ticker could be fascinating to you), while Bear contributing is increasingly about keeping your assets flawless for the long-run. Bear contributing is commonly finished with money related instruments, for example, shared assets, yet Bearmarket expects you to include a significant robust capital. Bear market is inalienably unsafe and you consent to expect total and full obligation regarding the results of all market choices that you make, including yet not constrained to loss of capital. None of the Bearmarket calls made by Mark Crisp and gathering organizations related with it ought to be interpreted as an idea to purchase or sell protections, nor guidance to do as such.

Bear market is a decent business for the individuals who can break down and take the correct choices to purchase or sell Bears at the correct occasions. Bear market isn't betting. Bear market isn't proper for everybody. There is a generous danger of misfortune related with market Bears. Bear market isn't so natural yet on the off chance that you get the correct tips than nothing is unthinkable.